Editor-in-Chief and Founder:
 *Lyndon H. LaRouche, Jr.*
Editorial Board: *Lyndon H. LaRouche, Jr. , Helga
 Zepp-LaRouche, Robert Ingraham, Tony
 Papert, Gerald Rose, Dennis Small, Jeffrey
 Steinberg, William Wertz*
Co-Editors: *Robert Ingraham, Tony Papert*
Managing Editor: *Nancy Spannaus*
Technology: *Marsha Freeman*
Books: *Katherine Notley*
Ebooks: *Richard Burden*
Graphics: *Alan Yue*
Photos: *Stuart Lewis*
Circulation Manager: *Stanley Ezrol*

INTELLIGENCE DIRECTORS
Counterintelligence: *Jeffrey Steinberg, Michele
 Steinberg*
Economics: *John Hoefle, Marcia Merry Baker,
 Paul Gallagher*
History: *Anton Chaitkin*
Ibero-America: *Dennis Small*
Russia and Eastern Europe: *Rachel Douglas*
United States: *Debra Freeman*

INTERNATIONAL BUREAUS
Bogotá: *Miriam Redondo*
Berlin: *Rainer Apel*
Copenhagen: *Tom Gillesberg*
Houston: *Harley Schlanger*
Lima: *Sara Madueño*
Melbourne: *Robert Barwick*
Mexico City: *Gerardo Castilleja Chávez*
New Delhi: *Ramtanu Maitra*
Paris: *Christine Bierre*
Stockholm: *Ulf Sandmark*
United Nations, N.Y.C.: *Leni Rubinstein*
Washington, D.C.: *William Jones*
Wiesbaden: *Göran Haglund*

ON THE WEB
e-mail: eirns@larouchepub.com
www.larouchepub.com
www.executiveintelligencereview.com
www.larouchepub.com/eiw
Webmaster: *John Sigerson*
Assistant Webmaster: *George Hollis*
Editor, Arabic-language edition: *Hussein Askary*

EIR (ISSN 0273-6314) *is published weekly
(50 issues), by EIR News Service, Inc.,
P.O. Box 17390, Washington, D.C. 20041-0390.
(703) 297-8434*

*European Headquarters:* E.I.R. GmbH, Postfach
Bahnstrasse 9a, D-65205, Wiesbaden, Germany
Tel: 49-611-73650
Homepage: http://www.eir.de
e-mail: info@eir.de
Director: Georg Neudecker

*Montreal, Canada:* 514-461-1557
eir@eircanada.ca

*Denmark:* EIR - Danmark, Sankt Knuds Vej 11,
basement left, DK-1903 Frederiksberg, Denmark.
Tel.: +45 35 43 60 40, Fax: +45 35 43 87 57. e-mail:
eirdk@hotmail.com.

*Mexico City:* EIR, Sor Juana Inés de la Cruz 242-2
Col. Agricultura C.P. 11360
Delegación M. Hidalgo, México D.F.
Tel. (5525) 5318-2301
eirmexico@gmail.com

# Europe and Africa In the New Silk Road

HELGA ZEPP-LAROUCHE IN ZHUHAI, CHINA

# The BRI and the Dialogue of Cultures: The Highest Expression Of Each Culture

*Schiller Institute President Helga Zepp-LaRouche gave a keynote address to the Maritime Silk Road conference in Zhuhai, in China's Guangdong Province, on Nov. 29. Her address has been edited.*

You, the Chinese people, find yourselves at a very decisive moment in history, and I know that after President Xi Jinping put the Belt and Road Initiative (BRI) on the agenda a little over four years ago, and the tremendous success of the policy of a New Silk Road since then, that you are completely aware of the extraordinary role China is now playing from the standpoint of the universal history of mankind. But let me share with you the view of a German—or actually, I see myself as an universal citizen, looking at what China is doing from the outside, from an international perspective.

For all the centuries up to now, from the earliest manifestations of human civilization, tribes, ethnic groups, nations or alliances of nations have pursued their self-perceived interests by various means—by negotiations, by diplomacy, and if this did not work out, by armed conflict and war. Geopolitics—the idea that a

LPAC TV

*Helga Zepp-LaRouche speaking in Zhuhai, China, Nov. 29, 2017, at a conference on international communications and Chinese (Guandong) companies going global.*

nation or group of nations has the right to pursue their interest against another group of nations—has led to two World Wars in the Twentieth Century.

It should be obvious to anyone, that in the age of thermonuclear weapons, war can no longer be a method of settling conflicts, if we as a human species are not to bring about our own annihilation. Humanity is distinct from all other species known in the universe so far, in that we are capable of creative reason. This means that we, unlike the animal species, can consciously change our mode of our existence, continuously discover new universal principles in science and culture, and develop a deeper and more profound knowledge about the physical universe, of which we are the most important part. So in a certain sense it is lawful that mankind would come up with the idea of how to overcome geopolitics, and establish a system of self-governance, which would guarantee the long-term survivability of humanity.

The concept of a "community of a shared future of mankind" presented by President Xi Jinping, is exactly that idea. By placing the notion of the one single mankind, defined from the standpoint of our common future, as the reference point for how to think about political, economic, social and cultural issues, President Xi has established a higher level of reason, a conceptual basis for a peace order throughout the planet. It is no coincidence that the concept for an entirely new paradigm in human history would come from China, as it is coherent with the 2,500 year-old Confucian tradition.

The economic dimension of this idea is expressed in the Belt and Road Initiative, the New Silk Road proposal which Xi presented in September 2013 in Kazakhstan. In the very short period of four years, this initiative for "win-win" cooperation has become the largest infrastructure program in history, developing six large economic corridors, numerous rail lines in Eurasia and Africa, ports, airports, industrial parks, power projects, water management, etc., with more than 70 countries participating. It is now twelve times bigger than the Marshall Plan in Europe in the reconstruction period after World War II, and it is open-ended. In Africa the "New Silk Road Spirit" has completely changed the outlook of the participating countries. For the first time after centuries of suffering from colonial oppression and a lack of financing, now, because of Chinese investments there is the perspective of overcoming poverty and underdevelopment in the near future. This has created an unprecedented sense of optimism.

At the 19th National Congress of the Communist Party of China, Xi defined the goal for China to become by the year 2050 "a strong, democratic, civilized, harmonious and beautiful country;" he defined the goal of politics to be creating a better and happier life for the people; he called on the people of all countries to work together to build a community of shared future for mankind—to build an open, inclusive, clean, and beautiful world that enjoys lasting peace, universal security, and common prosperity. Shortly after this remarkable event, the extremely successful state visit of U.S. President Trump to China signified a historic step in the effort to reach this goal.

With this global perspective for the next 33 years, President Xi Jinping put a vision on the agenda, which has inspired many people in many countries, especially in the developing sector, with an unprecedented spark of optimism. The response by some politicians in some Western countries, and by the mainstream media, has ranged from complete censorship of what President Xi actually said, to the wildest falsehoods concerning the real motives behind China's BRI policy. Some went so far as to say that China's policy represents a threat to the liberal order of the West. Does that mean that the idea of building a harmonious world, in which all nations can work together for the common aims of humanity, is a utopia, a dream, that can never become a reality?

I believe that the universal history of mankind can provide the answer to that question, because it shows that there are some profound characteristics, involving the ideal of the highest humanity, which are shared by the most noble expressions of different cultures. There is an amazing similarity among some of the most outstanding thinkers, who, coming from completely different cultural backgrounds, nevertheless come to the same insights into the nature of man and the purpose of mankind's existence. These philosophers, poets, and scientists have in common a fundamental optimism about the role of human beings in the universe, realizing that human creativity is itself a power in the further development of the physical universe, and that there is a cohesion between the harmonic development of all human mental and spiritual capacities, with the harmonious development of the state, as well as of states with each other, and also with the laws of the Cosmos.

In China, this image of man and harmony in the state and among states is associated foremost with Confucius and his 2,500 year-old tradition in Chinese culture, which accounts, in my view, for the gist of what is generally called "socialism with Chinese characteristics." Confucius has an image of man that perceives man as fundamentally good, with the obligation to tirelessly improve himself intellectually and morally, which he can do by exerting his inner will-power, and in aesthetical education through poetry, classical music and certain other arts. If the individuals develop themselves to become "*junzi*," there can be harmonious development in the family. If the government is run by *junzi*, the common good prospers.

The German "poet of freedom," as he is called, Friedrich Schiller, after whom the Schiller Institute is named, has an amazing affinity with Confucius, despite the fact that he lived and worked more than 2,000 years later. He, too, likewise develops the concept of the aesthetical education of man, as the only method for political progress, with a special emphasis on poetry and beautiful art. His notion of the "beautiful soul" is very similar to Confucius's idea of the "*junzi*." The beautiful soul, Schiller says, is someone who finds his freedom in necessity, does his duty with passion, and who has educated his emotions up to the degree that he can blindly follow his impulses, since they would never command him to do something which would be opposed to

Reason. Wilhelm von Humboldt, who created the best education system in the West, said about Schiller that he created a very special category, uniting philosophy and poetry on a higher level, as no one else had done.

Probably the closest almost-contemporary philosopher of Confucius in European culture is Plato, who likewise established a school of thought, which continued, albeit with many interruptions in terms of influence, through the centuries into the present. He also has the idea of a harmoniously ordered universe, in which development is embedded in the creation of the universe in such a way that it evolves from chaos to harmony, and where not only can man recognize that harmony, but can tune his own action in accordance with the laws of the universe for the sake of everyone. In his famous work *Timaeus*, he writes:

Participants at the Zhuhai conference.

> For God, desiring that all things should be good, and that, so far as this might be, there should be nought evil, having received all that is moving not in a state of rest, but moving without harmony or measure, brought it from its disorder into order, thinking that this was in all ways better than the other. Now it neither has been nor is permitted to the most perfect to do aught but what is most fair. Therefore he took thought and perceived that of all things which are by nature visible, no work that is without reason will ever be fairer than that which has reason, setting whole against whole, and that without soul reason cannot dwell in anything. Because then he argued thus, in forming the universe he created reason in soul and soul in body, that he might be the maker of a work that was by nature most fair and perfect. In this way then, we ought to affirm according to the probable account that this universe is a living creature in very truth possessing soul and reason by the providence of God.

This beautiful idea, that God created the best of all possible worlds, was explicitly elaborated by Gottfried Leibniz. In it each human being represents a monad, which has enclosed in it, in the small, all the characteristics of the universe at large—and there is an inclusive, pre-established harmony in that universe. The world is the best of all possible worlds, because it is constructed in such a way that every evil has the potential of generating an even greater good, which the human being can choose, because he or she has a free will. In that way, the degrees of freedom for the good increase, despite the existence of evil. From that follows the obligation of man to continuously ennoble himself in order to contribute to the progress of all of humanity and even the development of the entire cosmos.

To further this goal Leibniz created academies and scholarly societies, in order to gather the entire intellectual, scientific and cultural knowledge of all the people and put it to the service of all the nations. His conception was essentially the same as reflected in the new Center for the International Knowledge Development (CIKD), which will serve as a platform for nations to share ideas, so that their development is not delayed by the lack of access to new knowledge. That spirit influenced many scientists in history to give the fruits of their inventive power to that country which would make the best use of the discovery. One good example of that, is the collaboration of German scientists with China in the field of nuclear technology. Leibniz wrote to Czar Peter the Great, "I aim at the benefit of the entire human species, and I would rather accomplish a great good for the Russians, than a little for the Germans or the other Europeans, because my inclination and passion is the general best."

Leibniz was completely enthusiastic about China, about which he tried to learn as much as possible form the Jesuit missionaries. He was fascinated by the fact that the Kangxi Emperor had come to the same mathematical conclusions as Leibniz himself, and concluded from that, that there are universal principles accessible to all human beings and cultures. He even believed in the moral superiority of the Chinese, and wrote: "In light of the growing moral decay, it seems to be almost necessary, that Chinese missionaries be sent to us, who could teach us the application and practice of a natural theology. I therefore believe: that if a wise man were chosen to judge not the beauty of goddesses, but the excellence of peoples, he would give the golden apple to the Chinese." It is not surprising that Leibniz had a conception of the more advanced countries helping the less-developed, very similar to the New Silk Road idea.

In 1697 he published his book *Novissima Sinica*, about how Europe and China should cooperate to develop all countries located between them. He wrote: "Maybe it is the aim of the highest providence, that those nations which are highly civilized, but are located at the greatest distance, also uplift the peoples of the regions in between to a life more in accordance with reason."

Out of his optimistic idea of the best of all possible worlds, follows for Leibniz the right of the individual to the pursuit of happiness, a notion which has nothing to do with the hedonistic idea of "having a good time," but means the right to have a fulfilled life by developing the fullest creative potential for the benefit of the whole society. It was explicitly this Leibnizian notion which is included in the American Declaration of Independence, that all people have the inalienable right to "Life, Liberty and the Pursuit of Happiness."

But it was not only Leibniz who influenced the conceptions of the U.S. Constitution, the preface of which explicitly mentions the commitment to the common good—Confucius did as well. The intellectual father of the United States, Benjamin Franklin, was a convinced Confucian scholar. He published a treatise on the morals of Confucius in 1737 in the *Pennsylvania Gazette*, and he based his own moral philosophy, which he summarized in an outline of thirteen virtues, entirely on the morals of Confucius. So maybe the "good chemistry" which President Trump emphasized between himself and President Xi, given Xi's deep Confucian spirit, has something to do with the fact that President Trump has indicated repeatedly that he wants to revive the "American System," which is associated with the philosophy of the young American Republic.

To sum up the argument as to why—despite some present opposition in the West to the conception of a "community of a shared destiny of mankind"—there is nonetheless great reason for optimism that the beautiful vision will indeed become a reality, let me conclude with this. In all great cultures there have been thinkers who understood the deep connections between an optimistic image of the limitless moral and intellectual self-perfectibility of man, with the pursuit of the common good as the precondition for the long-term survival of society, and the cohesion between human creativity and the laws of the physical universe.

For a very long time these philosophers influenced their cultures independently from one another, sometimes living during the same period, but knowing nothing of each other, since it took years to travel from one country to the other. Sometimes they influenced one another over the centuries and beyond national boundaries. There was Plato, who influenced the Arab philosophers Al Kindi, Al Farabi and Ibn Sina, as well as the Christian thinkers Augustine, Nicholas of Cusa and Leibniz.

But one can also find an affinity of their ideas in the Indian Vedic writings or the scholars of Timbuktu. Without the exchanges between the Caliph Harun Al Rashid and Charlemagne, much of the cultural and scientific heritage of ancient Greece, Egypt, Spain, and Italy might not have been saved after the collapse of the Roman Empire.

As the ancient Silk Road led to an exchange not only of goods and technologies, but also of ideas and cultures, so will the New Silk Road lead to a sharing of the best expressions of human creativity for the benefit of the one humanity. Communication, travel and knowledge about each other have sped up tremendously and will continue to do so. What earlier was only stated by the greatest philosophers with metaphysical arguments about man and the physical universe, can now be proven by modern science.

And there is no better proof of the cohesion of the microcosm of the human mind and the macrocosm of the universe at large, than space research and travel. The fact that man can travel in space is the ultimate proof of the fact that an immaterial idea, an invention, a scientific breakthrough, has an effect in the physical universe, and can elevate the human species beyond any barriers of sense-perception. All the astronauts who have been to space report the same thing: that looking at the Earth from outer space, one does not see national borders, one only perceives the one human species.

So there is profound reason for optimism, despite the reluctance of some people in the West, that the beautiful vision of the One Dream of Mankind will come true.

# EIR Contents

www.larouchepub.com Volume 44, Number 49, December 8, 2017

*Mazeras Bridge, Mombasa-Nairobi standard-gauge railway, in Kenya.*

Xinhua/Chen Cheng

# The International Conference of The Schiller Institute On November 25-26, 2017

### by Alexander Hartmann

Nov. 28—The new paradigm of the Belt and Road Initiative, launched by China, is an invitation to all countries to cooperate in major new infrastructure projects for reconstruction and economic development, and to increase human productivity through investment in new energy technologies, science, and space travel. This new paradigm moved another step forward on Nov. 25-26, at an international conference of the Schiller Institute in Frankfurt, Germany.

The Institute was founded by Lyndon LaRouche and Helga Zepp-LaRouche to win Europe to the cause of reconstruction of the Middle East and Africa. At this conference, more than 200 participants from over 30 nations, heard high-level speakers from Eastern and Western Europe, China, the United States, Africa, and the Middle East, who described the economic and cultural potential of the new paradigm, and presented their common commitment to its complete success.

Zepp-LaRouche's keynote address and the first two panels were covered in detail in the Dec. 1 *EIR*. (Also see the conference program below.) Here we present a brief overview before providing the content of the final two panels, on Europe's role in the Belt and Road, and on future scientific and technological breakthroughs, respectively, for our readers.

In her opening speech, the chairman of the Schiller Institute, Helga Zepp-LaRouche, referred to the statement of the philosopher Gottfried Wilhelm Leibniz that we live "in the best of all possible worlds" because the universe is always able to further perfect itself. Therefore, mankind is challenged to overcome great evils by even greater goodness.

The strategy of the New Silk Road offers a chance to overcome the obvious lack of development that her husband Lyndon LaRouche—who was among the participants—has for 50 years been addressing with his proposals for a new, just world economic order. Since President Xi Jinping's announcement of the New Silk Road as the official policy of the Chinese government in 2013, we see this idea materializing more and more, at the Belt & Road Forum for International Cooperation in Beijing last May, and at the 19th Congress of the Chinese Communist Party in October, where overcoming poverty was declared a goal—people should be given a better life, not only in China itself, but throughout the world.

The geopoliticians of the old paradigm claim that all this is merely Chinese propaganda, but they cannot hide the fact that their own old system is falling apart, while China's strategy, with its development corridors, railways, and diplomacy in Eastern Europe, Ibero-America, and Africa, is making tremendous strides.

President Trump's recent China visit is also very important, as the world's two largest economies have set themselves the goal of "extending peace and prosperity to all other nations," as President Trump said in China. This is also a reason for hope for economically distressed regions in the United States, such as West Virginia, whose governor welcomed Trump's diplomatic success in China: now infrastructure and industry in his state can be rebuilt thanks to massive Chinese investment.

Trump's talks with Xi and Russian President Putin, Putin's cooperation with Xi, and in particular the meeting of Putin with Syrian President Assad, and China's development projects in Africa, are signs of hope.

Concerning Africa, one must acknowledge the foresight of Lyndon LaRouche, who wrote as early as 1980 that the genocide in Africa must be ended by a new political paradigm based on the ideas of Leibniz and Hamilton—the combination of science and statecraft to promote contributions of creative individuals for the benefit of all. Increasing population density and energy flux density, through technology transfer and labor force development, would ensure that every child born has the chance to make a creative contribution to the progress of humanity as a whole.

Europe in its present state is on the opposing side, but it could and should change this by accepting Leibniz's prognosis that China and Europe can cooperate to the benefit of the world, due to the affinity between their philosophy and culture, in which the Confucian concept of *ren* corresponds to the Christian *agapē*. Many aspects of this affinity can be found in Xi's politics. Europe is suffering from the brainwashing by the Congress for Cultural Freedom (CCF) which occurred following Roosevelt's death, which—as the German daily *Frankfurter Allgemeine Zeitung* has recently admitted—created the left-liberalism of "political correctness" that today dominates Western thinking. The creation of the CCF coincided with Churchill's proclamation of the Iron Curtain, McCarthy's witch-hunt, the Truman doctrine, and George F. Kennan's thesis of the "necessary lie"—the forerunner of today's fake news and false "human rights" campaigns. The CCF managed the destruction of classical music and art, through the attacks by the Frankfurt School on beauty and idealism, and their cult of atrocity.

The Schiller Institute, she emphasized, has always advocated a cultural and scientific renaissance in the tradition of the *Coincidentia Oppositorum* of Nicholas of Cusa and the striving for harmony of Confucius, who both insist on uniting the many contributions of all for the good, as in a contrapuntal fugue in music. Such a new renaissance is necessary to overcome the destruction brought on by the CCF, so that neoliberalism will disappear forever, as did scholasticism in the Middle Ages.

# FULFILLING THE DREAM OF MANKIND

Nov. 25-26, 207, Bad Soden/Taunus, Germany
**SATURDAY, NOV. 25, 10 A.M.-6 P.M.**

MUSICAL OPENING: Mo Li Hua (Jasmin Flower),Chinese Folk Song—Arr. Benjamin Lylloff
*Schiller Institute Chorus; 1st Violin: Caroline Hartmann; 2nd Violin: Odile Mojon; Viola: Claudio Celani; Cello: Athil Hamdan; Conductor: Benjamin Lylloff*

CONFERENCE KEYNOTE

- The New Silk Road, a New Model for International Relations
  *Helga Zepp-LaRouche, President and Founder, Schiller Institute*

Panels I and II were covered in the Dec. 1 issue of *EIR*.

## PANEL I: The Earth's Next 50 Years

- KEYNOTE: President Xi's Perspective for the Year 2050 and the Perspective of African Development
  *Prof. He Wenping, Chinese Academy of Social Sciences, Director of African Studies, Beijing*
- Integration of Egypt's Transportation Plans 2030 with the New Silk Road Project
  *Dr. Saad Mohamed Mahmoud Elgioshy, former Transport Minister, Egypt*

- The Trump Administration—Impending Economic Policies and Media Discord
  *George Lombardi, former Social Media Consultant to President Trump*
- A Future for Europe After the Euro
  *Marco Zanni, Member of the Economic and Monetary Committee, European Parliament*

13:00-14:00   LUNCH BREAK

## PANEL II: The Need for Europe to Cooperate With China in the Industrialization of Africa and the Middle East; Transaqua as the Rosetta Stone of the Continent's Transformation

- Extending the New Silk Road to Southwest Asia and Africa: A Vision of an Economic Renaissance
  *Hussein Askary, Schiller Institute, Southwest Asia Coordinator, Stockholm*
- Italy-China Alliance for Transaqua
  *Franco Persio Bocchetto, Foreign Director, Bonifica S.p.A., Italy*

- The Need for Europe to Cooperate with China in the Industrialization of Africa
  *Mehreteab Mulugeta Haile, General Consul of the Federal Democratic Republic of Ethiopia, Frankfurt am Main*
- Egypt's 2030 Mega-Projects: Investment Opportunities for Intermodal and Multimodal Connectivity
  *Mrs. Moni Abdullah, Executive Manager of Pyramids International, Cairo*

8 P.M. CLASSICAL CONCERT

### SUNDAY, NOV. 26, 2017—10 A.M.-6 P.M.

Panels III and IV are covered in
this Dec. 8 issue of *EIR*.

### PANEL III: Is Europe the Continent of Poets, Thinkers, and Inventors, or on the Sidelines of Strategic Developments? An Optimistic Vision for the Future of Europe

- KEYNOTE: What Europe Should Contribute to the New World Paradigm
  *Jacques Cheminade, former Presidential Candidate, France*
- China's Initiative: From the Doom of Self-Destruction, to Prosperity and Progress: A View from Ukraine
  *Dr. Natalia Vitrenko, Doctor of Economics, MP (1994-2002), Chairwoman of the Progressive Socialist Party of Ukraine*
- One Belt One Road—An Opportunity for Development in the Western Balkans
  *Dr. Jasminka Simić, Author and Journalist, Ph.D., Research Fellow, Editor-Journalist of the Radio-Television of Serbia, Belgrade, Serbia*

- Bulgaria's Contribution to the B&R Initiative in the Context of the Geopolitical State of the Balkans
  *Prof. Mariana Tian, Institute for Historical Studies, Bulgarian Academy of Sciences*

13:00-14:00   LUNCH BREAK

MUSICAL OPENING: Ganymed, Franz Schubert (Text: Goethe)
  *Leena Malkki, Sweden—Soprano; Werner Hartmann—Piano*

- China's Belt and Road Initiative and Its Long-Term Impact on African Countries
  *Dr. (Cand.) Alexander Demissie, Founding Director, The China Africa Advisory*

### PANEL IV: The System We Live in Is Not Earthbound— Future Technologies and Scientific Breakthroughs (Transportation, Thermonuclear Fusion, International Cooperation in Space Research)

- KEYNOTE: The Scientific Method of LaRouche
  *Jason Ross, Science Advisor, Schiller Institute, U.S.A.*
- Energy Transition—from Bad to Worse
  *Prof. Dr. Helmut Alt, University of Applied Sciences (Fachhochschule), Aachen*
- Current Situation of High Temperature Gas-Cooled Reactor in China
  *Wentao Guo, Paul Scherrer Institute, Switzerland*

CONCLUDING DISCUSSION

# Is Europe the Continent of Poets, Thinkers, and Inventors, or on the Sidelines of Strategic Developments? An Optimistic Vision for the Future of Europe

## JACQUES CHEMINADE: PANEL III KEYNOTE

# What Europe Should Contribute To the New World Paradigm

*Jacques Cheminade*

*Jacques Chminade is a former French presidential candidate. This is an edited transcript of his presentation to the Nov. 25-26 Schiller Institute Conference, "Fulfilling the Dreams of Mankind."*

*Qui sommes-nous?* Europe and the nations of Europe, who are we? Who are we? Europe. "Of course one can jump up and down on one's chair like a kid goat, bleating 'Europe, Europe, Europe,' but it leads nowhere and signifies nothing." These were the provocative words of General de Gaulle, in an interview given on December 14, 1965. Even today, some still maintain that in reacting in that way, de Gaulle was only concerned with France's own political Grand Design and its prestige, while others claim that he was mainly inspired by commercial and economic, especially agricultural motivations, in a conception of protectionist national interests raised against all other nations. Both are wrong.

It is now key for European nations to ask themselves why it is wrong—because that raises the question of what a nation-state and what a world region like Western Europe really are. This is the first question to raise in order to muster a sense of a mission, to realize what we could and should contribute to the new world paradigm, to our World Land-Bridge. Identifying the source is indeed key to understanding what could and should spring from it. All the more so, as it was the same de Gaulle, who after recognizing the People's Republic of China in January 1964, declared quite prophetically what nobody else was then able to foresee: "It cannot be excluded that China will once again become what it was for centuries, the greatest power in the universe."

What de Gaulle rejected was a supranational institution and a pseudo-federal model of integration launched against the very principle of nation-states. He understood that solidarity, as opposed to what is happening in the current European Union, means having a common mission, not to undermine national sovereignties, but to base solidarity on a mutual understanding. He told his press secretary, Alain Peyrefitte, the following: "What the Anglo-Saxons want is a Europe without shores, a Europe that would no longer have the ambition to be itself. A Europe without borders. Europe *à l'anglaise* [English style].... A Europe in which every European country, beginning with ours, would lose its soul."

The key word here is "soul." Because if Europe can contribute today to the New Silk Road and the World Land-Bridge, it is with the soul of each and all of its nations, the soul of its major composers, poets, philosophers and statesmen, with their science, their art and their technologies, and not with the sterile product of an artificial entity ruled by a monetarist bureaucracy. De Gaulle, in that sense, was definitely and absolutely pro-European. In the same interview about the "kid goats," so often misquoted, he said:

"As long as I am French, I am a European. Given the fact that we are here in Europe—and I would have to say that France has always been an essential if not a capital part of Europe—therefore I am of course European.... Our countries have their history, their language, their way of life, and they are French, German, Italian, British, Dutch, Belgian, Spanish, or Luxemburgers. These are the countries that we have, to progressively become accustomed to live together and act together. In that sense, I am the first one to recognize and think that our Common Market is essential, because if we manage to

*Charles de Gaulle*

organize it, and consequently to establish a real economic solidarity among these European nations, we will have done a lot for the fundamental coming together of the people and for our common life."

And he added, in a speech given in Bonn on June 11-12, 1965:

"We Europeans are builders of cathedrals. It took us a long time. We have made many efforts. But we have succeeded.... In any case, there is a foundation—it is the reconciliation of France and Germany. The pillars are our six members of the European Economic Community. There is going to be a top, made of the arches and the roof, and it is going to be our political cooperation. The pillars are built after the foundation is laid. The top is going to be settled when the pillars will have been properly built.... When our cathedral has been built, it is going to be opened to others. Who knows if, with them, when we will have acquired a taste for building, we are not going to build an even greater and more beautiful cathedral, the union of the whole of Europe?"

De Gaulle, in the middle of World War II, on November 11, 1942, had already invited "Europeans to join together in a practical and lasting fashion."

It is key to understand this concept. Of course, things have changed a lot since the 1940s and 1960s of the last century, but the challenge remains the same and is even clearer. There are two traps. The first is to think that there is way out that leads to the past as such, as a withdrawal of a nation into itself, a fixed model. The second is to subjugate our nations to a European Union which has become a tool of a one-world monetarism, ruled by money fakers such as Mario Draghi, through the euro and the financial institutions of the fake Europe and NATO. Both mean submitting to the ruling financial oligarchy, the ideology and financial power of the British Empire with its somehow Anglo-American new skin, which is the very reason why de Gaulle vetoed British admission to the European Union.

It is very important for our American and Chinese

*The signing of the Declaration of Independence.*

friends to understand this point: It means that Europe must break away from geopolitical rule to be truly itself, and European nation-states must work together for common projects, and therefore not give in to that geopolitical rule, one-by-one or together. It should be clear that the present-day European Union is based on a betrayal of the best historical and cultural sources of Europe—and I mean sources, not roots clinging to the ground. But it should also be clear that the European nations and their leaders, and their so-called populist opponents as well, have also given away their souls. Therefore, where is hope? What could our European contribution be? It obviously lies in the sense of an understanding of what a nation-state is, something which is latent, even if concealed, in the hearts of all true Europeans. Our task is to inspire an awakening from the sleep of reason.

A nation-state is much more than a territory or a given state of the population, or even a religion or a tradition. It is the dynamics of an idea evolving and increasing in power and scope over the course of history. Friedrich Schiller, Heinrich Heine, François Rabelais, Miguel Cervantes, Dante Alighieri, Alexander Pushkin, Percy B. Shelley or, at their best, Adam Mickiewicz and Victor Hugo brought forth this "idea" in their writings, as many poets did in their own ways. This idea is dynamic, as all ideas are, and its political embodiment, I am convinced, is the best contribution that we can make to the new world paradigm.

If you are inspired by this idea, you begin to understand the Confucian tradition of China, and you won't fall into the traps of geopolitics or monetarism. Great minds always tend to coincide over the main issues. In the Treaty of Westphalia of 1648, we have the conception of the "advantage of the other," and in the American Declaration of Independence, we find the "pursuit of happiness," which is the same conception of happiness developed by President Xi Jinping—a happiness that it is only possible to reach for oneself if you make it possible for others.

To have something to contribute, demands that we Europeans all engage in a profound heart-searching, since the path to reason is opened by the heart. Such an effort by us, understood by the Chinese, would be the best way to respond to the challenge of the Belt and Road Initiative. To build, out of the present European Union, the euro, and NATO, a true Europe of the nation-states, as de Gaulle said, "from the Atlantic to the Urals." And this time building well beyond the Urals, to connect the Atlantic with the China Sea on the one side, and to a renascent America on the other, should and would be an education for the world, and the basis for the great World Land-Bridge. Such an effort would take us out of the ideology that says that success can only be achieved at the expense of the other, with the expectation that the winner takes all. And the Chinese would appreciate that. It would also get us out of the foolish idea that the New Silk Road is good because it is a tool against the United States. And the Chinese could appreciate that.

## Europe's Proper Role

President Trump's visit to China proved that the Chinese authorities are committed to a community of development among all nations, because they understand that their interest coincides with the interests of all of them. Here in Europe, we should work to surpass the cultural pessimism of geopolitics and financial greed, and revive those moments, such as in our great Renaissance, when we attempted to contribute to creating a Republic by reaching out to the shores of America, to free ourselves from the grip of the European oligarchy. In that sense, we can contribute by reappropriating our own history and rediscovering how we brought about our revolutions in science and art.

It also demands shedding a self-destructive euro-centrism, to bring to the world the gift of a true internationalism, freed from both narcissistic nationalism, and from the cosmopolitanism of financial slave-herders. Then, we can understand and joyfully share with others the fact that Europe was only able to exist because, between the fall of the Roman Empire (despite the reign of Charlemagne), and our great Renaissance, remarkable achievements took place in other parts of the world. Mainly in China, but also in India, Cambodia and parts of Africa. In that sense, to make our contribution fruitful, we must understand that our civilization has sources other than the Greek and Judeo-Christian. This does not mean underrating those fundamental, great Judeo-Christian contributions, but, on the contrary, realizing that they are not only key for the world of the future, but also substantial for us now.

Schiller Institute

*Helga Zepp-LaRouche (lower right) and other participants on May 14, 2017, at the opening session of the Belt and Road Forum for International Cooperation.*

Europe has not only been made from within European territory. For example, if it were not for the visitors from China who came to meet Paolo dal Pozzo Toscanelli at the time of the 15th-century Council of Florence, America would probably not have been "discovered" by us Europeans until much, much later—and the cause of freedom against the oligarchy would have been, at least temporarily, lost.

Today, the Belt and Road Initiative, together with the existence of the BRICS, is not only a network of infrastructure projects, economic institutions and high-speed trains, but a change of paradigm which is not only Chinese—although inspired by China—but universal, as the Chinese understand much better than we do. It is a potential leap from a geopolitical and financial order based on the possession of goods and territory, to an economic order of exchanges and mutual development, based on connections and permanent innovations, and not on annexations and possessions. To understand this, we should contribute and share with the Chinese the approach of Gottfried Wilhelm Leibniz on this point.

Starting from the principle of the universality of reason, Leibniz, at the end of the 17th century, notably in his *Novissima Sinica*, not only concludes that Christian revelation theology and the Chinese natural theology of Confucianism are compatible, but that it is necessary to launch economic, scientific and cultural cooperation between the two "more developed extremes of Eurasia," Western Europe and China. He writes:

"A specific arrangement of Providence, according to my opinion, has ordained that the highest culture and ornament of the human race, are today somehow concentrated at the two extremities of our continent, Europe and China; the latter as the Europe of the Orient embellishes the opposed side of the Earth."

Leibniz considers the Europeans more advanced in the science of non-physical things and in metaphysical speculations, and in geometry, considered from the standpoint of philosophy, while the Chinese have a better management of practical philosophy and the rules of life. Hence the Belgian Jesuit Ferdinand Verbiest taught the "European sciences," trigonometry and astronomical mathematics, to the Kangxi Emperor, so much so that the Emperor became a highly learned man, looking at geometry from the standpoint of philosophy and not mere artisanry, and composed a book to promote the principles of such a beautiful science to children.

The Jesuit priests sent to China by the French monarch were organized by Leibniz to share this knowledge more generally with a Chinese literate elite, with the communication of ideas accompanied by the exchange of goods. But for Leibniz this was not a one-way relation. He points out, both seriously and ironically, that "The state of affairs among us seems to me such, through the overflow of corruption, that it would seem almost necessary that the Chinese should send us missionaries to teach us the use and practice of natural theology, as we send them some to teach them the revealed theology."

Europe should contribute to deepen the knowledge, on both sides, of this first draft of a global Silk Road, as a web of both physical and mental exchanges. A good lesson for us all is to understand how this mission was historically killed. First, by the ultra-montanists of Rome, who refused to admit that the *ren* and the *li*, the idea of a sovereign universal good, could be compatible with the spirit of Christianity—and second by the brutal assault of the British Empire, supported, as Victor Hugo denounced this, by the French, notably through the Opium Wars and murderous "gunboat diplomacy" and plunder.

*Artist's rendition of the deployed CFOSAT spacecraft in orbit.*

This shared historical knowledge should contribute to avoid repeating the mistakes of the past; to then, always, consider our relations with the eyes of the future.

There are of course many areas of cooperation now, but in a far too limited way. On the history of sciences, looking to the input we Europeans can have, there is the common study of the works of Vernadsky, the German and Russian schools of cosmic and astronomic sciences, the Italian school of hydrodynamics, and the French developments in laser fusion.

Concretely, there is a lot to share, provided there is a political will and not ideological mistrust. I have been told so many times, that if scientists organize their own channels of communication, they work very happily together because science does not belong to one single country, but to all of us, to build a better world. But the problem in all ventures is the lack of collaboration from the European administrations, which, too often, think in terms of the Chinese situation of five to ten years ago, without taking into account the enormous progress accomplished in China in the most recent years. The French seem to be even more bureaucratically paralyzed than the Germans: There are presently about 5,000 Chinese doctoral students in Germany, but only 500 in France. The last Franco-Chinese science commission took place six years ago, and there have been fewer than five visits by heads of scientific agencies from either side in the last ten years! The worst is the censorship of many initiatives by the security and defense services on our side, and the lack of a long-term strategy of cooperation.

France does have, for example, two aerospace projects with China: CFOSAT, a satellite to be launched in 2018 for the observation of the oceans; and SVOM, set for 2020, for the observation of gamma-ray pulses. The French project Cardiospace has been embedded in the Tiangong 2 Chinese space mission.

But all of this is far, far away from what we could and should contribute. I am fighting for the launching of areas of common and far-reaching cooperation, on the Franco-Chinese and European-Chinese levels—for a truly ambitious space policy, the blossoming of an oceanic "blue" economy, and the development of Africa.

None of that can be decided or arranged, at a French or European level, from the bottom up. A strategy from the top down, vertically promoted within an *Auftragstaktik* approach, is needed to contribute in a crossroads-type of exchange of ideas, research, innovations and goods, which has to be reached to establish a community of development and world peace. For us, as Europeans, the emergence of China presents the opportunity to open our eyes, look at ourselves, and lift our heads—instead of walking on them. It will make us happier, like all those Chinese children driven by joyful curiosity, and all those we have seen from the Yemeni youth cabinet.

The challenge for us adults is to care for them, being rationally and wholeheartedly proud of our nations once again, proud to work together for a future based on a community of principles, solidarity and peace.

Let us stop crawling egotistically from the past—and we do crawl egotistically from the past in Europe—and leap ahead toward the future to rediscover and recover our souls, the souls of Europe and of our nations. It is for us, true Europeans and true patriots, to make our mandatory contribution, inspired by our past history of world citizens. It is time now to be human, fully human, as partiots and world citizens.

NATALIA VITRENKO

# China's Initiative: From the Doom of Self-Destruction, to Prosperity and Progress

*Below is the presentation of Natalia Vitrenko, Doctor of Economics, People's Deputy of Ukraine in the 2nd and 3rd Convocations (1994-2002), and leader of the Progressive Socialist Party of Ukraine, at the Nov. 25-26 Schiller Institute Conference. This is an edited translation of her presentation.*

The existing world order is past its time. As long as it continues, mankind will be threatened by a spread of the conflicts in the Middle East, Ukraine, and North Korea into a nuclear Third World War, and by a crash of the worldwide speculative financial

*Natalia Vitrenko*

system, which will be just as destructive. The international institutions of globalization, created by the leading capitalist countries under the aegis of the U.S.A.—the International Monetary Fund, the World Trade Organization, NATO, the World Bank, and the European Bank for Reconstruction and Development (EBRD)—have failed to solve a single one of the most acute problems facing mankind: hunger, the inaccessibility of medical care and education for billions of people, drug addiction, trafficking in human beings and their organs, and rampant terrorism on every continent of our planet. That is why 15,000 scientists from 184 countries issued their second Warning to Humanity on Nov. 13, 2017, (the first was in 1992), identifying global

threats and proposing ways to solve them.

In this setting, reasonable people cannot fail to understand the need for a radical change in the paradigm of international relations and the model of globalization. In the course of history it has come to pass, that China has proposed the new paradigm. This ancient, five-thousand-year-old civilization, which has creatively adopted the newest model of a socialist economy.

The People's Republic of China, with the largest population on Earth, severe income inequality between regions, low standards of living, and economic and military backwardness, has been able within an unbelievably short period of time, to transform into a mighty agro-industrial power. Its GDP has surpassed that of the United States. China is ahead of the U.S.A. and the EU in the rate and scale of its development. China is not only confidently exploring outer space, with its ambitious lunar program, but is also showing the entire world indisputable successes in solving social problems. Whereas five years ago 100 million people were still living in deep poverty in China, as of 2017 only 43 million were, and by 2020 deep poverty will be eliminated, according to the Communist Party of China plans.

Chinese leader Xi Jinping is actively strengthening international ties, finding new markets for Chinese goods, production of which is growing at the fastest rates in the world. The Chinese government has a clear interest in building solid economic alliances and good diplomatic relations. This requires a constructive ideology of development, with cooperation instead of merciless competition, intrigues, and financial speculation.

This was the background to China's initiative, put forward by Xi Jinping in September 2013, to create the economic model of the New Silk Road, under the slogan "One Belt, One Road," on an unprecedented scale. The project anticipates $3 trillion in investments, and already encompasses around 100 countries on various continents. The Chinese President reported these parameters at the special Belt and Road Forum, held in Beijing in May 2017. Taking part in the Forum were the heads of state or government of more than 30 countries, leaders of national and international public institutions, and businessmen—over 1200 participants in all. By 2030, Xi promised, the project will have been built. This will be a transformation of civilization, a change of the world for the better.

Does the world community need this? Yes, with great urgency. That is why it is so important for government officials, politicians, experts, and people's diplomacy to support the Chinese initiative.

Will there be (or, rather, are there already) opponents of this initiative? Without a doubt there are, and there will be. The apologists of the old world order will fight against it with all their might. After all, the current system of globalization creates comfortable conditions for financial speculators of all stripes, drug traffickers, corrupt officials, war-hawks representing the world's most powerful military-industrial complex, and the terrorists they breed.

One weapon in their arsenal of means for destabilizing the situation on various continents is the creation of suicide-states—countries that self-destruct—destroying their own sovereignty and economic foundation, their population, and their science and culture, in order to foster hotbeds of tension, zones of bloody conflict, and to draw enormous resources into provoking and waging wars. In such countries, power is held by armed agencies (both those of the state and non-governmental ones), which drain the budgets of their own countries and condemn their people to unimaginable suffering.

A vivid example of this struggle by the old world order against the new is Ukraine.

It was no accident that precisely in the Autumn of 2013, when the world heard Xi Jinping's announcement of the New Silk Road project, the coup d'état began in Ukraine. The whole world now knows that this unfolded according to the plans, under the direction, and with the powerful informational, financial and organizational support of the United States.

The result of the policies adopted in Ukraine after the coup, namely integration into the European Union and NATO and moving towards war with Russia, all completely under the outside guidance of the U.S.A., caused great harm.

GDP. Real GDP, according to World Bank figures for 2014-2016, fell by one-half, to 50.9% of its 2013 level. Even the projected 2% GDP growth in 2017 will increase it by only 1 percentage point against the 2013 level (to 51.9%).

I should note that the liberal economic model, implemented since 1992 according to the IMF's prescriptions and with its loans, had already earlier been ruinous for Ukraine. With a real GDP of $261.9 billion in 1990, Ukraine was one of the top ten countries in the world in per capita GDP. As of 2016, real GDP stood at only one-third of the 1990 level ($93.3 billion). The past three years have dealt an even more crushing blow, through the crash deindustrialization of the country.

Key to this process was the ideology of "Eurointegration" for Ukraine, which led to the signing of Ukraine's Association Agreement with the EU in 2014, the disruption of production cooperation with Russia, and the loss of the huge Russian markets for the output of Ukrainian factories. Entire sectors of our national economy have been lost as a result: rocket-building, ship-building, the aircraft industry, and the automotive industry. Machine-building was the powerful core of industry in Soviet Ukraine, comprising 30.5% of total industrial output in 1990. As of 2013 this share had fallen to 10%, and by 2016—to 5.8% of a total industrial output which itself has fallen by 25% since 2014. Economists estimate that if the current policy continues, machine-building will account for no more than 2% of industrial output in 2020.

In this setting, of course, there has been a steep increase in unemployment and in the number of workers leaving the country. Even before the fighting in the Donbass, more than 4 million people had left to seek work in Russia, and more than 2 million had gone to EU countries. The coup d'état, the war in southeastern Ukraine, mass political repressions, and crash deindustrialization have all contributed to a large outflow of the population. With the introduction in June 2017 of visa-free travel to the EU, this will only increase. Let me give the example of Poland: in 2013, there were 9,800 Ukrainian citizens working in Poland on formal labor visas. In the first quarter of 2017, this number had increased tenfold, to 98,000. In addition, around 1 million Ukrainians are working in Poland on temporary work permits. Polish Minister of Foreign Affairs Waszczykowski has said that 1.3 million visas with the right to work were issued to Ukrainians in 2017, and in 2018 half again as many will be issued!

And that's without mentioning how many of my fellow citizens are forced by want and unemployment to flee to Czechia, Hungary, Germany, Spain, Slovakia and other countries!

*Obama's Assistant Secretary of State, Victoria Nuland, with Ukrainian President-elect Petro Poroshenko.*

That is because the conditions of life at home are becoming more and more unbearable.

In these three years, our national currency (the hryvnia) has been devalued by a factor of almost three-and-a-half (from 8 hryvnias to the dollar, to 26.5 hryvnias to the dollar). According to government statistics, prices in Ukraine rose by a factor of 2.72—nearly triple—in the same period of time. It is clear that foreign capital gains a lot from this kind of devaluation of our labor power, of Ukraine's industrial output, and of our natural resources. There is covert and overt looting going on, a merciless, humiliating exploitation of Ukraine's workers.

Look at the changes in the monthly minimum wage. Even though prices and rates were rising out of sight, the minimum wage in 2015-2016 stood at only half the value it had in 2013. Only on January 1, 2017 was it raised slightly (to 3200 hryvnias, or $123), which is still 20% below the 2013 level. The overall wage system in Ukraine has become horribly distorted. Top executives of the national gas company Naftohaz, the National Bank, Ukrainian Railways, etc., have monthly salaries of hundreds of thousands or even millions of hryvnias (tens of thousands of dollars), while the overwhelming majority of working people eke out a miserable existence on $100 or 200 per month. People are forced to harm their health and deprive themselves of leisure and vacation time, while working two or three jobs to support their family. Or to forego having children. Or to flee the country.

The situation of pensioners is even worse. The monthly minimum pension established by the Euromaidan regime has remained at less than half the 2013 level throughout these years. One-half of the 11.8 million pensioners in Ukraine receive that minimum level. And the pension reform adopted last month, as demanded by the IMF, has only made the situation worse, in effect raising the pension age, reducing the actual amount of each pension, and depriving millions of employees of their pension benefits.

That is why the population of Ukraine is dying off at horrific rates. Ukraine ranks first in Europe in 2017 in the level of mental illnesses and the death rate. According to official statistics, out of the 52 million population of Ukraine in 1990, only 42 million remain. But, contrary to the international practice of taking a census once every ten years, no census has been conducted in Ukraine since 2001. That is deliberate. The regime does not want to answer for the genocide, and they want to be able to commit vote fraud by registering millions of dead souls. Economists estimate, based on levels of bread consumption, that no more than 25 million people live in Ukraine today. Since 6 million of the decline in population is accounted for by the loss of Crimea and those living in the self-proclaimed Donbass republics, this means that Ukraine has lost 21 million people since 1990 through emigration and the excess of deaths over births.

The 2017 United Nations Human Development report notes that Ukraine fell from 50th place on the Human Development Index in 2015, to 84th place in 2016.

The Gallup Institute in the United States this month published a study ranking Ukraine as one of the three countries with the highest "suffering" rates in the world, alongside Haiti and South Sudan. The survey showed that only 9% of the population in Ukraine consider themselves to be thriving, 41% are suffering, and 50% are somewhere in between.

One of the factors in the suffering of the Ukrainian population is the insane rise of residential utility rates.

The increase of household gas rates in the past three years, is a good example. These rates have nearly tripled! Yet on Nov. 3, 2017, the IMF imposed four new conditions for disbursing the next tranche of its loan to Ukraine. One of them is to raise household gas prices for the population once again. This is despite the fact that Ukraine has its own natural gas production (around 20 billion cubic meters annually), which fully covers the needs of the population! One of the Euromaidan leaders, Arseniy Yatsenyuk, loudly denounced the previous government on this count, promising that gas prices would be brought down sharply. Brought down, indeed! As prime minister of Ukraine, Yatsenyuk forgot about his promises, but not about increasing his own net worth.

President Petro Poroshenko likewise forgot about his promises. He renamed the fratricidal war in southeastern Ukraine as the "Anti-Terrorist Operation" (ATO), which is an absolutely wrong definition, and promised to end it within days. Instead, it has gone on for three and a half years!!! According to United Nations figures from May 2017, more than 10,000 people have been killed, including 3,000 civilians. In addition, tens of thousands have been wounded or injured, and more than 3 million have fled the region as refugees, going either to Russia or to other regions in Ukraine.

Government spending on the military is now 5% of annual GDP. Estimates of the awful cost of rebuilding from the tremendous destruction of the Donbass have already reached $50 billion! That is equal to two-thirds of Ukraine's budget for 2018! Rather than forcing Kiev to carry out its part of the Minsk agreements of February 2015, which after the UN Security Council resolution of Feb. 17, 2015 became a document of international law, mandatory for all parties to implement, the U.S.A. and the leading EU countries are closing their eyes to the bellicose position of the Ukrainian regime, which I assert has a direct interest in continuing the bloodbath. That is because if the war ends, then the Ukrainian regime would have to rebuild the infrastructure and factories of the Donbass, which it destroyed, and answer to the population, above all the people of Donetsk and Lugansk Regions, for failing to meet the government's social obligations, and for genocide against the people of Ukraine.

Every public opinion survey shows that at least two-thirds of the population of Ukraine demand an end to the war in the southeast of our country. But there are other forces, who preach the misanthropic ideology of Nazism. These include various neo-Nazi parties, movements, volunteer battalions, and non-governmental organizations. They are generously financed by Ukrainian oligarchs and sponsors in the West, while the Presidents and other leaders of the U.S.A. and EU countries close their eyes to the overt fascism. These people do not hide their positions or their ideology! They have named streets and avenues not only in Kiev, but all over Ukraine, after their idols Stepan Bandera, Roman Shukhevych and Yevhen Konovalets, who were collaborationists and agents of German Military Intelligence, the Abwehr. The slogan "Glory to Ukraine—to the heroes glory" had been adopted in April 1941 at the Second Grand Assembly of the terrorist Organization of Ukrainian Nationalists, the OUN(b) (which at that time was allying with Hitler to fight the USSR), as a call-and-response like "Heil Hitler—Sieg Heil." In Ukraine after the Maidan coup, it was made an official greeting.

Today's Nazis are completely unrestrained—they are not merely taking advantage of the conditions of lawlessness, but are also sponsored by the regime—and they wreak havoc throughout the country. They organized the blockade of coal from the Donbass; they use the methods of raiders to seize banks, companies, stores, and offices of businesses and political parties; they cause the cancellation of tours by artists they don't like; they pressure the courts in a daringly blatant way; and they beat up peaceful demonstrators, thus terrorizing the entire population of the country. Our party, the Progressive Socialist Party of Ukraine, and I personally as its leader, have experienced this directly.

I would like to take the opportunity to offer my sincere thanks to all our friends from the LaRouche movement and the Schiller Institute, who in various forms—articles, statements, demonstrations, and a parliamentary inquiry in the European Parliament—have supported our party's fight for a progressive transformation of the world, and for turning Ukraine into a democratic and prosperous nation.

In October 2017 it became known that Ukraine, despite everything, will join the New Silk Road project by allowing Chinese freight trains to cross its territory en route to the European Union countries, and through the importation by China of food products including flour, candy, vodka, cooking oils, and so forth. As a citizen of my country, a politician and a scientist, I was sincerely happy to hear that Ukraine would not be isolated from this project of the century.

Unfortunately, however, I also understand that in a country that is falling apart, with a backward economy, a population being brutalized, and the rampaging of armed bands, there is a threat that any serious international projects will be wrecked. And what if bands of neo-Nazis seize Ukraine's nuclear power plants or major chemical factories? What will happen to the transport corridors and the cargoes moving through them? Therefore the normalization of the situation in Ukraine, an end to the fratricidal war, the elimination of paramilitary groups, and a ban on the neo-Nazi ideology and any parties and movements which preach it— all these steps are needed immediately not only for Ukraine itself, but for the entire world community that strives for progress and development.

Only then will this black hole on the Eurasian continent be eliminated. Then, conditions will be created for restoring a firm economic foundation for Ukraine and for creating millions of new, modern jobs, conditions for the return of the emigrants to their country, for steady growth of incomes and the quality of life for the population, and for the full-fledged inclusion of Ukraine in a new, progressive model of world civilization, where, as China proposes, there will be:

**peace instead of war, cooperation instead of competition,**
**respect instead of humiliation,**
**plenty instead of hunger.**

JASMINKA SIMIĆ

# One Belt One Road—an Opportunity for Development in the Western Balkans

*Below is the presentation of Jasminka Simić, Ph.D.,[1] to the Nov. 25-26 Schiller Institute Converence, "Fulfilling the Dream of Mankind." This is an edited transcript of her presentation.*

Thank you Mr. Chairmen, Jacques Cheminade, also for your memory on the glorious and deep French-Serbian friendship!

Dear colleagues, I would like to express my deep gratefulness to the Schiller Institute, especially Mrs. Helga Zepp-La-Rouche and Mr. Lyndon La-Rouche, and also Mrs. Elke Fimen, for inviting me to this conference which has

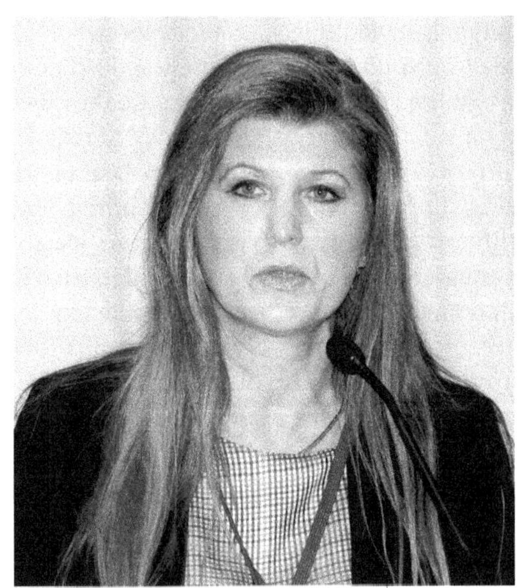

*Jasminka Simić*

gathered together distinguished experts to discuss the global world situation and the role of China's One Belt, One Road project in this process. Also, I will emphaisize that my late husband Prof. Dr. Predrag Simić, professor of the Faculty of political Science at the University of Belgrade, was an eminent Balkan expert and European sinologist who maintained contact with the Schiller Institute and Mr. Dean Andromidas.

Serbia is a part of Southeast Europe, the Western Balkans region, which also includes Montenegro, the Republic of Macedonia, Bosnia and Herzegovina, and Albania. All of the countries are on the euro-integration or euro-Atlantic path; at the same time, they have a more than 60-year long history of relations with the People's Republic of China. The strategy of

1. Research Fellow, Editor-Journalist of the Radio-Television of Serbia, RTS, Belgrade, Serbia

the mega project One Belt, One Road (renewed old Silk Road) and economic cooperation between China and the countries of Southeast Europe on the platform of the "1+16" policy have a short-term and a long-term challenge. In the short term, growing trade and investments from China are welcomed to mitigate the consequences of the economic crisis and to stabilize Southeast European economies. In the long term, China's interest in investment in transport infrastructure in Southeast Europe might add to and compensate for structural investments from the EU, via its Instrument for Pre-Accession Assistance (IPA) which have diminished since the emergence of the eurozone crisis.

## The Origins of the Partnership Between Southeast Europe and China

I would remind you that the history of relations between China and the countries of Southeast Europe which have gone through three stages:[2]

1. The first stage lasted from the forming of the People's Republic of China, 1949, until the second half of the 1970s when China established diplomatic relations and developed economic ties, but the overall relationship was ideologically driven and shaped by the framework of the Cold War and the Sino-Soviet dispute.

2. The second stage lasted from the 1970s until the 1990s, with normalization of relations (as a consequences of the Sino-Soviet dispute), first with Romania and Yugoslavia, followed by other countries in the region, as part of China's policy of "Four modernizations" and its opening up to the world. It was during the 1972-73 period when China signed air traffic agreements with Romania, Yugoslavia, and Albania, opening a transcontinental southern air route linking Beijing, Belgrade, Bucharest, and Tirana. While China's relations with the countries of Southeast Europe throughout this period were politically driven, after the fall of the Berlin Wall and the end of the Cold War, economic interests gradually moved to the fore. Numerous Chinese immigrants arrived in this region in the 1990s and opened their small and medium-sized businesses. In the mid-1990s some Southeast European countries made modest investments in China but these attempts ended in failure.

3. The third stage began in 2000 when the Chinese economic presence in Southeast Europe was growing with the arrival of large Chinese investments. The most important thing for this region was China's decision to rent the Greek port of Piraeus as the main entry point for China's goods into Europe, emphasizing the new perspectives that came with the mega project "One Belt, One Road."

After having opened the doors of the European Union at the European summits in Zagreb (2000) and Thessaloniki (2003) to all the countries of the Western Balkans, political stability enabled these countries to start the process of transition to market economies, multiparty democracy and the rule of law. In such circumstances, foreign investments began to arrive in the region, and Southeast Europe recorded higher rates of economic growth in the period from 2000 to 2008. The global economic crisis, primarily the eurozone crisis, has hit these countries. The first wave of the eurozone crisis was 2009-2011, but the second wave of the eurozone crisis that began in Greece in 2011 spilled over to all these countries, except Turkey (part of Southeast Europe) and hit the region hard. The entire region saw a decline of growth rates, negative economic growth, and high unemployment rate, while EU austerity measures significantly reduced European investment in the region.

In that period, China became one of the ten largest trading partners for all the countries of Eastern and Southeast Europe.[3] The value of trade between China and Southeast European countries increased from $3 billion in 2000 to $53 billion in 2013 and, according to Chinese estimates, by 2018 its value will again double. "Unlike the 1990s, when China's activities were based on small and medium-sized companies of Chinese immigrants, in the last 17 years some big Chinese investors started to come to the region. They strongly influenced development of the region's infrastructure and production capacity."[4] China's new approach to Central

---

3. China was focused on so-called green-field investments in Central and Eastern Europe. The largest Chinese city in the Balkans was opened in Afumati (2011), near Bucharest, where there were approximately 1,240 shops spreading over 40 acres. The "Chinese Dragon Trade Centre" in Belgrade and the "Chinese Centre" in Zagreb were open in 2010. Loïc Poulain. China's New Balkan Strategy. August 2011. Centre for Strategic & International Studies, Central European Watch. Volume 1, Number 2.

4. See: Predrag Simič, *Odnosi NR Kine i Jugoistočne Evrope: Kontinuitet i promena*, Zbornik radova povodom 40 godina sinologije "Biseri sa zrncima pirinca 1974-2014," str. 18., Filoloki fakultet u Beogradu, Beograd, 2015.

---

2. See: Predrag Simić, *Odnosi NR Kine i Jugoistočne Evrope: Kontinuitet i promena*, Zbornik radova povodom 40 godina sinologije "Biseri sa zrncima pirinca 1974-2014," Filološki fakultet u Beogradu, Beograd, 2015.

*Pupin Bridge in Belgrade, Serbia, constructed by China Road and Bridge Corporation (CRBC), was China's first big infrastructure investment on the European continent.*

and Eastern Europe was announced in the speech of former China Prime Minister Wen Jiabao in Warsaw in 2012. He presented China's "12 Measures for Promoting Friendly Cooperation with Central and Eastern European Countries." This document contains a series of short- and medium-term measures to improve China's economic relations with the 16 countries of the region, that include a $10 billion credit line. The aim is to quickly dispatch China's trade and investment missions to Europe in order to boost the trade and inject new investments into the region. It became known as "1+16" policy—China and 16 countries of Central and Eastern Europe, as a part of China's global project "One Belt, One Road" or "New Silk Road." This is China's vision of forming a mutually-dependent economic and political community, that would stretch from East Asia to West Europe, just like the Old Silk Road established some 2,000 years ago, during the Han dynasty, enabling goods and information to be moved towards the rest of the world, i.e. to the West.

In addition to the economic front, China's initiative includes cooperation in other areas: cultural cooperation, closer educational relations by providing scholarships including Chinese language courses, and tourism through cooperation between the China Tourism Administration and similar institutions in Europe, to increase the number of Chinese tourists in the region in the framework of the "people-to-people" policy. The Faculty of Philology at the University of Belgrade enrolls up to 35 students per year. Adding the post-graduate students to that amounts to a total of 350. Serbia has become increasingly attractive for Chinese tourists. In 2016, 18,409 Chinese tourists arrived in Serbia, while the number of overnight stays totaled 42,986. Similar data are also valid for the region of Southeast Europe. For example, the number of Chinese tourists visiting Greece was 12,203 in 2012, and in 2013 that number more than doubled to 28,328.

As part of this development thrust in the region, China announced new investments in transport infrastructure in Southeast Europe, including the modernization of the railway between Belgrade and Budapest, and a highway through Montenegro from the Serbian border to the port of Bar on the Adriatic. In Macedonia, Chinese companies have been building the highway between the capital Skopje and the major tourist resort at Lake Ohrid. Before that, in 2009, the Chinese company, Dongfeng, struck an agreement with Serbian truck maker FAP to assemble vehicles in Serbia; in Bulgaria—a part of Southeast Europe—Chinese Great Wall Motor opened a car factory.

Further steps towards better and deeper cooperation were provided by the summits of the Prime Ministers of China and the 16 countries of Central and Eastern Europe, which was held in November 2013 in Bucharest, and next in December 2014 in Belgrade. The following summits were in China (2015) and Latvia (2016), and the present one which is now underway in Budapest (2017).

## Present Day Serbia-Western Balkans-China

Serbia and China signed an important strategic partnership agreement in August 2009, which consisted of a wide array of subjects, including the mutual respect of territorial integrity, plans for trade development as well as cultural, technological, and scientific exchanges.[5]

---

5. Statistical Office of the Republic of Serbia, Dissemination and

Serbia's exports to China are mainly machinery, plastics, and wood products, and in 2016 its value amounted to $25.3 million, while imports from China amounted to more then $1.6 billion, mostly high technology products.[6] According to present plans, the trade volume between the two countries will soon reach about $3 billion. China is increasingly interested in importing organic food, agricultural tourism, and scientific innovation, while it will continue to develop industry, information technology, and small- and medium-sized enterprises.

Serbia was among the first countries to be given a $10 billion credit line. The first investment was for the construction of the Mihailo Pupin bridge in Belgrade (Borča-Zemun), built by the China Roads and Bridges Corporation (CRBC). China is building a two-section segment of the corridor 11 highway, Horgoš to Požega, which leads from the north to the west of the country. China's Export Import Bank is financing the construction of the third block of the thermal power plant Kostolac B and the reconstruction of the thermal power plant Nikola Tesla, near Belgade. China also is ready to finance the modernization and reconstruction of the Belgrade-Budapest railway. Serbia has began construction work on the section of this railway from Novi Sad to the Hungarian border. The new high-speed train between Belgrade and Budapest will be a future China-Serbia joint project.

China's Hesteel steel company bought Serbian Železara steelmill in Smederevo, for 46 million euros in 2016. The Bank of China opened its branch in Serbia in January 2017, becoming China's first bank to start operations in the country, with operations extending over the entire Western Balkan region. The Bank of China will make further contributions to China's Belt and Road Initiative through its financial services in the region. The flight from Belgrade to Beijing reopened in September.

For Southeast Europe, where Serbia is located, the most important initiative is the Chinese 21st Century Maritime Silk Road project, with its starting point at the Greek port of Piraeus. China's largest shipping com-

Xinhua/Ju Peng

*Zhang Dejiang, chairman of the Standing Committee of China's National People's Congress (NPC), visits a steel mill during his official friendly visit to Serbia, July 17, 2017.*

pany, COSCO, in 2008 signed a 35-year concession agreement with the seaport of Piraeus, and bought a 67% interest in the port. COSCO is also among the bidders to rent the port of Thessaloniki in northern Greece, a major transport hub on the Balkan Peninsula. China is interested in building a port on the Danube in Belgrade, a confirmation that this river is both the water corridor and geostrategic framework of political and economic cooperation between China and Europe. Serbia and China have signed a Memorandum of Cooperation on this project. It will include the harbor and the dock. The Danube is the best way to connect this part of Southeast Europe, passing through Bulgaria to the Black Sea, to continue through to Turkey, and to the Middle East by rail. Serbia is a milestone of the New Silk Road, as Chinese President Xi Jinping said during his visit to Belgrade 2016.

## EU References to the Cooperation Between China and Southeast Europe

The distance between Beijing and Belgrade is about 7,400 kilometers, but during the last few decades, despite that distance, the situation in the Balkans was more visible to China than to the European capitals. Chinese investments in Southeast Europe bring a financial incentive which is especially important in the period of economic crisis, and the present crisis in the Eurozone, in particular. Serbia, Bulgaria, Romania, Montenegro, the Republic of Macedonia, and other


Public Relations Division, Available from: http://www.pks.rs/MSaradnja.aspx?id=73&p=1&pp=2 &, 22 November 2017.

6. Statistical Office of the Republic of Serbia, Dissemination and Public Relations Division, Available from: http://www.pks.rs/MSaradnja.aspx?id=73&p=1&pp=2 &, 22 November 2017.

Xinhua

*Serbian Prime Minister Ana Brnabic attends the launch of work on the first part of a 34.5-km stretch between Belgrade and Stara-Pazova in Serbia, to be carried out by China Railway International.*

countries, recorded a growth of trade with China, and in Chinese investments in 2013. On the other hand, the EU and the U.S.A. think that Chinese investment can help to stabilize the economies of Southeast Europe, but they also fear that in the future it could create new divisions within the EU, undermining its Common Foreign and Security Policy (CFSP). This apprehesive thesis is supported by the fact that China's investments in South and Southeast Europe in recent years have been growing faster than investments in other parts of Europe, although their level is still modest compared with investments in Western Europe. China has emphasized that the cooperation with the countries of Central and Eastern Europe on the 1+16 policy platform is in accordance with the China-EU comprehensive strategic partnership, and expresses readiness to continue cooperation based on mutual respect.

The European Union has been investigating the high speed rail project that is part of China's One Belt\ One Road project to connect Serbia's capital, Belgrade, with Budapest, Hungary. The EU is assessing the financial viability of the $2.89 billion railway project, and is investigating whether the project violates EU procurement laws that require public tenders for large transport projects. An EU observation addressed to Hungary, charging that this project has not been carried out in accordance with EU rules because there was no tender, because EU rules demand that China as a partner can not be both the creditor and the contractor. Hungary, as the EU member state, is subject to the full rigour of European procurement law, while Serbia, as a candidate state is subjected to looser rules. Upgrading the 350 kilometer Budapest-Belgrade railway into a high-speed rail link is expected to shorten travel time between the two capitals from eight hours to three.

The president of the European Commission, Jean-Clauder Juncker announced the EU plan, in his State of the Union speech to the European Parliament in September 2017. The EU plan will screen investments of all foreign takeovers in the EU in sensitive industrial sectors. This act is being observed in China as possible political pressure from Europe against China. President Junker was supported by French president Emmanuel Macron, who announced that he intended, in cooperation with Germany, to take a conssesion in the port of Thessaloniki, Greece, instead of China.

## Conclusion and Recommendations

Cooperation with China is especially important for EU-member countries in Southeast Europe and non-EU countries in the region of Western Balkans. China's infrastructure projects can boost better regional economic cooperation, and the process of euro-integration of the region. The main problem in the Western Balkans is their lack of infrastructure (i.e. lack of direct airlines, inadequate road and railway networks) which minimizes the concept of regional cooperation and creates a fear, that the region will remain just a location on the map, which will never be transformed by concrete solutions.

The main problem for future cooperation of the Sino-Western Balkan countries, is to create a mechanism for harmonizing Chinese investments in the region with the eurointegration process of these countries. As candidates for EU membership, these countries have to harmonize their policies, especially foreign policy, with the EU and its Common Foreign and Security Policy (CFSP). Their relations with China should follow the EU policy towards China. That will be the main challenge for the implementaion of the One Belt One Road project in the future. As for Serbia, the same goes for its cooperation with Russia, especially because of its refussl to impose economic sanctions on Russia, as the EU and U.S.A. did in 2014. But, Serbia and the Western Balkan countries have a chance to capitalise on their position in the New Silk Road in order to develop their economies.

Since I'm a scholar and journalist, I would like to emphasize that the media in the countries along the Belt and Road should support and encourage any kind of cooperation which can lead towards a better economy and life, both with the EU and with China.

Thank you for your attention!

PROF. MARIANA TIAN

# Bulgaria's Contribution to the B&R Initiative in the Context of the Geopolitical State of the Balkans

*Mariana Tian, Ph.D., is Associate Professor at the Institute for Historical Studies of the Bulgarian Academy of Sciences. This is the edited text of her address to the International Schiller Institute conference on "Fulfilling the Dream of Mankind," Nov. 26, 2017, in Bad Soden/Taunus, Germany, which she presented under the title, "Bulgaria's Contribution to the B&R Initiative in the Context of the Geopolitical State of the Balkans." Some subtitles have been added.*

*Mariana Tian*

Dear organizers, dear colleagues,

From the European geopolitical point of view, the Balkans have always been a region difficult to understand and to rule. They are an important connection point between Europe and Asia. The land infrastructure is most commonly associated with trade routes to the Middle and Far East.

Nowadays the Balkans continue to have some problems, but the breezes of change—and to a better future, if I dare to say it—have started to blow again. Some of the contributing factors to this improvement and increased intensity of relations among the Central and East European (CEE) countries are related to the Chinese initiatives "16 + 1" and "Belt and Road."

I would like to stress a few key points here:

• The West Balkans are something like the hot topic of the future. Even for our Presidency of the Council of the European Union (EU) next year, Bulgaria will have the West Balkans as a priority in regard to future EU enlargement plans.

• Nevertheless, we should not forget the importance of the East Balkans, because they have their geopolitical strengths: big harbors on the Black Sea, political and economical stability, they are already members of the Union and a final frontier.

• Only united—by analogy with Chinese philosophy of harmony and peaceful development—will the Balkans progress and step ahead.

As Prof. David Gosset of the Academia Sinica Europaea in Shanghai noted in the Fifth Euro-China Forum, Bulgaria is a key component of the Black Sea system. This system has traditionally connected the two edges of Eurasia. It was a part of Marco Polo's journeys on the Silk Road. Nestorian Monk Rabban Sawma, envoy of China's Emperor, also crossed it. The Black Sea system has an important role to play in the construction of a more cooperative Eurasia.

The geopolitics of the wider Black Sea region sug-

gests that it will be important for the development of the Silk Road Economic Belt, which spreads over this territory.

On this path is the Europe-Caucasus-Asia Transport Corridor. Part of it is the connection between the Georgian and Bulgarian (and also Romanian) seaports, respectively: Poti (Georgia), Varna and Burgas (Bulgaria), and Constanta (Romania).

## The Sea2Sea Corridor

The continuation from the Bulgaria seaports to other corridors is being strategically addressed at the moment. Our Prime Minister, Boyko Borisov, and the Transport, Information Technology, and Communications Minister, Ivaylo Moskovski, have signed a memorandum for a rail transport corridor with Greek Prime Minister Alexis Tsipras and his Infrastructure, Transport, and Networks Minister, Christos Spirtzis.

This event expresses the political willingness of Bulgaria and Greece to create a transport corridor on the Aegean Sea-Black Sea-Danube axis. Named "Sea2Sea," the project will develop the transport corridor concept by executing connections between the Greek ports of Thessaloniki, Kavala, and Alexandroupoli (on the Aegean Sea) to the three Bulgarian cities of Burgas and Varna on the Black Sea and Ruse on the Danube, through railway links. It would be a full multi-modal corridor in compliance with the core Trans-European Transport Network (TEN-T as they call it), so it could possibly get finance through the Juncker Plan and the European Investment Bank. A few of the important benefits of this corridor are these:

• Alexandroupoli has become a strategic port, which provides a fast connection to Burgas and Varna and, according to the experts, the cost of the railway transport will be much lower in terms of dues.

• It will bypass the Bosphorus and Dardanelles straits in Turkey and will reduce the travel time from two days to six hours. Of course, this is not only about time; the situation in Turkey is not as easily predictable as in the past, so the construction of this corridor is strategically supported.

• The Ruse-Varna connection will increase the benefits, because it will give access not only between the seas, but also to one of the main transport arteries of Europe—the Danube river.

The tentative cost of the project in its Bulgarian section is around 1 billion euro and about 4 billion for its counterpart in Greece. The transport facilities are supposed to be built within 10 years or so.

The Danube strategy will also play a part in defending the project proposal.

## Pan-European Corridor VIII

Another important corridor that goes from the Bulgarian Black Sea coast is the Pan-European Corridor VIII. In this regard, the recent development in the relations between Bulgaria and Greece could also be seen as something positive. There is a political will to strengthen the ties between the two states, which is ar-

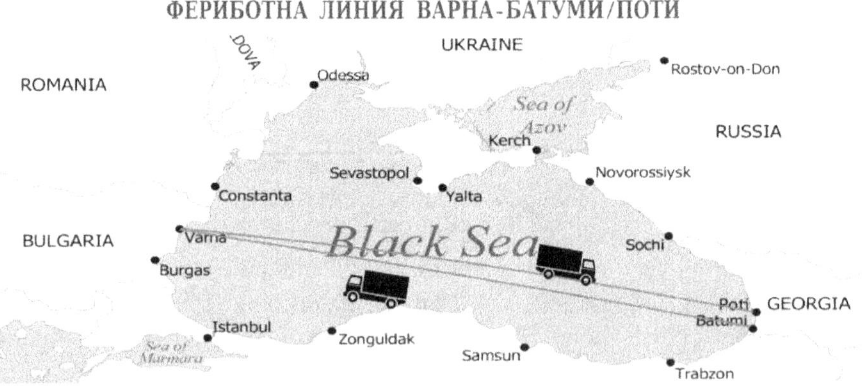

ticulated with the signing of the Treaty of Friendship, Good-Neighborliness, and Cooperation. This act was necessary and will boost infrastructure cooperation as well as cooperation in other sectors.

Most important, it is another step toward finally starting working on Corridor VIII.

The corridor will link the Black Sea and Adriatic Sea via Bulgaria, Macedonia, and Albania. This link was too long postponed for different reasons, but will be of great benefit in the development of the countries on this East-West axis. During the meeting in July with Macedonian Prime Minister Zoran Zaev, our Foreign Minister, Ekaterina Zaharieva, said that building Corridor VIII will be a high priority for both countries.

Just to mention, last month during the third Cultural Cooperation Forum between China and the Central and East European Countries (CEEC) in Hangzhou, Bulgaria did the right thing (as did other countries in the 16+1 initiative) in supporting the establishment of a China-CEE cultural coordination center in Macedonia.

I will get back to this corridor in a moment.

**Bulgaria-Macedonia.** Bulgaria and Macedonia will build the rail link between Sofia and Skopje (through Kyustendil and Gyueshevo, and it must be completed by 2027).

The government has approved a memorandum of understanding between the Ministry of Transport, Information Technology, and Communications of the Republic of Bulgaria, and the Ministry of Transport and Communications of the Republic of Macedonia, on the development of the railway links between Sofia and Skopje.

The Bulgarian State is committed to the construction of the railway link between Sofia and Pernik-Radomir-Macedonian border by 2027. Macedonia is in charge of the construction of the segment Kriva Palanka-Deve Bair-Bulgarian border by the end of 2025.

**Bulgaria-Albania.** Albania, the other concerned party in this initiative, is also experiencing a boost in bilateral relations with Bulgaria. The government in Tirana voted for the amendments to the Minority Pro-

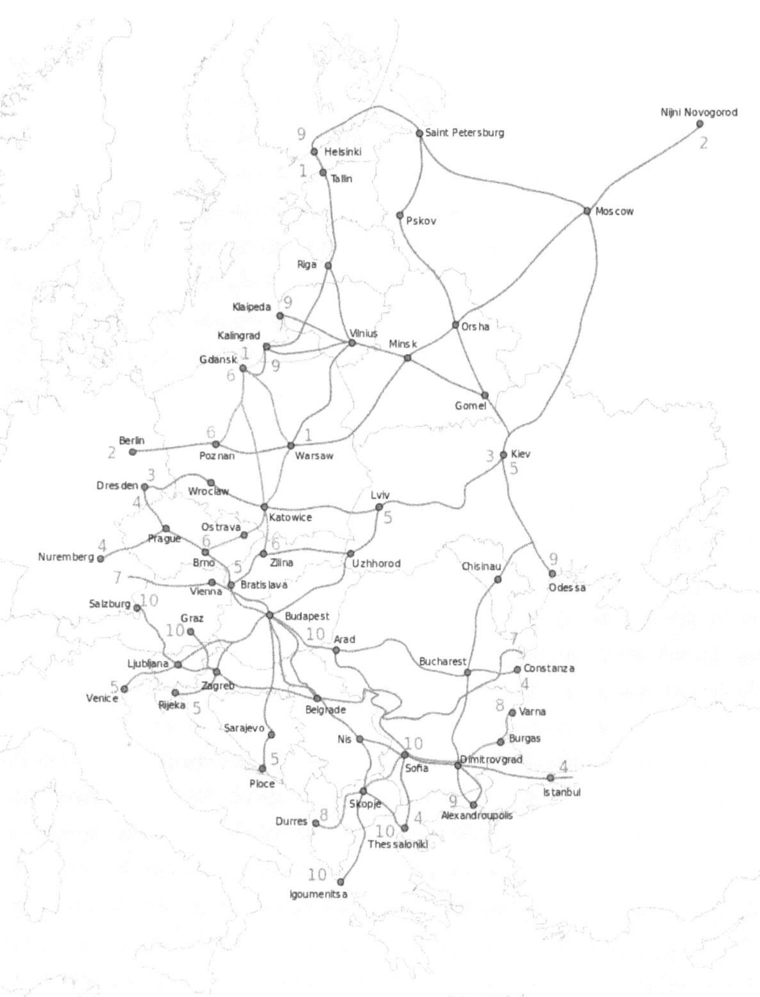

tection Bill, approved by consensus in the country's parliamentary legal committee, identifying that there is a Bulgarian minority, and now it is officially recognized by Albania.

**Bulgaria-Serbia.** After Serbia built new sections of the highway from the city of Nish, the connection between Bulgaria and Serbia is getting better. In this regard, a good boost in Bulgaria will lead to the Parliament voting for the launch of a toll roads system, which should come into action in 2018. This will untie the hands of the goverment when they are proposing projects for big investors, and Chinese companies have already expressed interest in this sector in Bulgaria.

## Corridor VIII in Relation to Sea2Sea

I will give my expert opinion on Corridor VIII, because there are some controversies over it. There is a belief that the signing of the Sea2Sea memorandum of understanding with Greece in Kavala, on September 6, was intended to block the realization of the Corridor VIII project. I dare to say that Sea2Sea and Via Egnatia are not mutually exclusive. [A significant part of Corridor VIII follows the ancient Roman road, Via Egnatia, which went from Italy to the Black Sea and Constantinople. Today this route is called Via Egnatia, Egnatia Odos, or the A2 motorway. —ed.]

Here are some facts:

• In northern Greece, the direct railroad connection from Thessaloniki to Igoumenitsa is still to be constructed, as is the Thessaloniki-Kavala-Xanti line.

• The same is the case with Florina (Lerin) in Greece, to Pogradec (Ohrid Lake) and Durrës port (on the Adriatic), both in Albania.

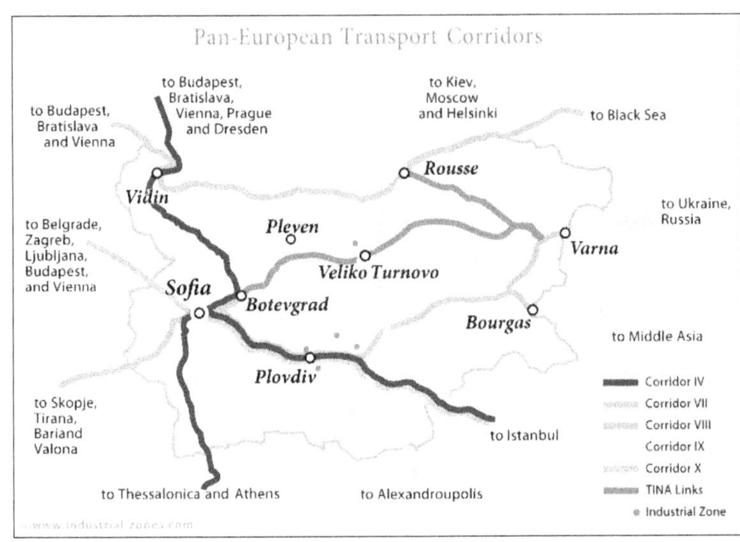


• With some small exceptions (Thessaloniki-Plati), the railroad is not electrified in northern Greece from the border with Bulgaria at Svilengrad to the Ionian Sea.

• In many places there are no railway lines at all, and wherever they are, all are one-way [single track]. The modernization of Ormenio-Alexandroupoli has not been accomplished. Only partial rehabilitation of Thessaloniki-Florina has been done.

The situation of railroad transport on Corridor VIII is as follows:

• Bulgaria is working on the modernization from Burgas to Sofia, with more than two-thirds of the distance being a two-way electrified line. After that, Gyueshevo should be upgraded and electrified from Radomir to the border.

• In Macedonia, new sections should be built from Kumanovo to Gyueshevo, and from Kichevo to the border with Albania. These sections are much shorter than those of the corridor Egnatia. Kumanovo-Gyueshevo will be funded with money from the European Commission and the European Investment Bank (EIB). The remaining route from Kumanovo to Kichevo is for modernization.

• In Albania, the entire, existing route from Drach to Ohrid Lake and the border is for modernization.

This leads to the following overview:

• At first sight, Greece has a significant advantage over Bulgaria, Macedonia, and Albania, because A2 is entirely ready for the southern neighbors and next year Greece is expected to complete the rehabilitation of Ormenio-Ardanio/A2.

• On the other hand, if we analyze, the highway route from Burgas to Dupnitsa (through Sofia) is ready in Bulgaria, [while the] Dupnitsa-Gyueshevo connection remains. To the west, there is a ready route from Kumanovo to Gostivar and it has been built from Kichevo to Struga (Ohrid). Kumanovo-Gyueshevo remains, [as also] Gostivar-Kichevo and the detour to Kiafasan and the Albanian border.

• In Albania the highway from Durrës (Drac) to Tirana is ready and is being built next to Elbasan, which should soon be completed. It remains [to be built] from Elbasan to Kefalasan.

Igoumenitsa is much further from Bari and Brindisi (both in Italy) by sea than the Albanian port of Durrës, and if the destination is southern Italy, even now the time from Bourgas along Corridor VIII is less than that of Egnatia.

If the destination is Gibraltar/Atlantic Ocean, then from Bulgaria one travels from Bourgas to Kulata to Igoumenitsa on the Struma Motorway, and again, even in terms of the still unfinished A3 route, it is faster on Corridor VIII in Bulgaria than on A2 in Greece.

If the destination is the Suez Canal/Indian Ocean, you can still use the Trakia Highway in Bulgaria to Thessaloniki and Athens, instead of Egnatia.

Lastly, if the destination is Kavala or Alexandroupoli on the Aegean Sea, then the route goes naturally through Svilengrad. The same arguments apply equally to Varna and Ruse.

Whatever Greece does, it cannot stop Corridor VIII, and it will be gradually built.

This concludes my review of the Balkans with respect to the 16+1 and Belt and Road initiatives. Thank you for your attention!

# China's Belt and Road Initiative and Its Long-Term Impact on African Countries

*This is an edited transcript of the presentation by Dr. Alexander Demissie of Ethiopia to the Nov. 25-26, 2017 Schiller Institute Conference, "Fulfilling the Dream of Mankind."*

I'll begin with two or three words about myself, so you can understand why I'm here. My background is in international relations. I'm a PhD holder in China-Africa relations, and have been studying China-Africa relations since 2003, so I am quite aware of what has been happening over the last decade in this area.

*Alexander Demissie*

Today, I will try to discuss with you the Belt and Road Initiative (BRI), and how it is connected to Africa. What kind of long-term impacts are we expecting when we are talk about the BRI and Africa?

This is a map I always use in my presentations. I always ask my audiences "What do you see here?" It's a very simple question. You should see something. It's a rhetorical question. I'm not expecting you to answer. It usually takes several minutes until people realize what they see here. What you see is the absence of the American continent. [laughter] You see that the Chinese vision of the BRI is absolutely Eur-Asian oriented. Starting in China, it is primarily Eur-Asian oriented. The idea of the BRI, probably even your idea back in the 1970s, is the Land-Bridge, which we have also been discussing yesterday and today.

Within this map you will see Africa. Africa is prominent. It is not entirely in the center, but is on the left side, and should be part of the BRI idea. We know that Africa is a late-comer. It's an after-thought in China. It was not a primary address for the BRI. Therefore, it took people such as Professor He and Professor Justin Yifu Lin from Peking University to bring Africa into the picture. Starting in 2013-14, they were the first ones writing about Africa and that Africa should be considered as part of the BRI. They coined the term "One Belt, One Road, One Continent," to include the African continent. Later we will see that we cannot even talk about the African continent.

How do we understand the BRI from the African perspective? We see that the BRI is a very open and over-arching idea. It is open in that anybody can come in, and "dock" with it. Earlier we heard about the 16+1 initiative in the Central and Eastern European countries. This is one such idea. If it's good or bad, that's another discussion.

## China's Belt and Road Initiative

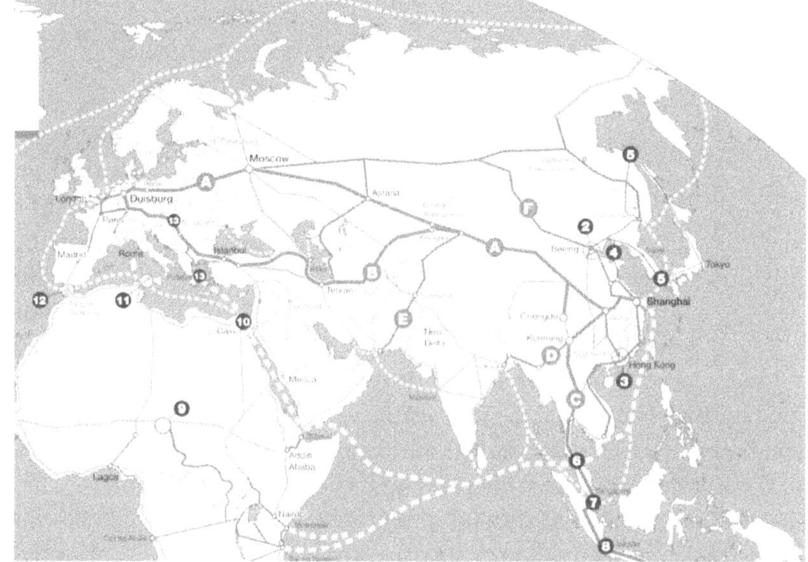

## How do we understand BRI in African context?

- It is primarily Eurasian oriented project (*Africa is latecomer*)

- It is an overarching & open idea providing new narratives (*re-writing of history and creation of new voices*)

- It is primarily infrastructural undertaking without political institutionalization (*fits into current African needs*)

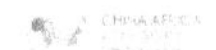

## "The Africa We Want"

AU Agenda 2063: Plan for structural transformation

Infrastructure development as aspiration for "connected infrastructure vision"

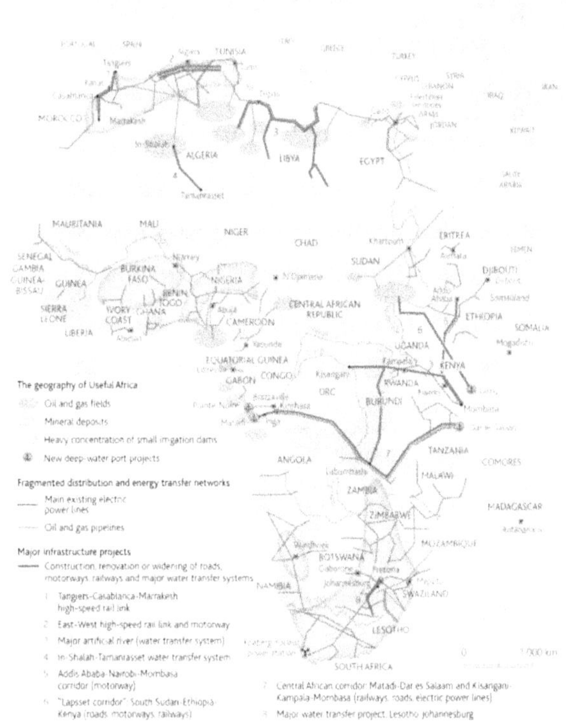

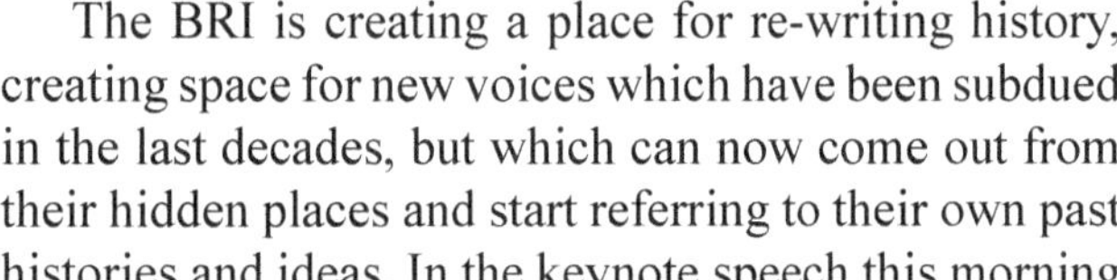

The BRI is creating a place for re-writing history, creating space for new voices which have been subdued in the last decades, but which can now come out from their hidden places and start referring to their own past histories and ideas. In the keynote speech this morning

## BRI enhances existing FOCAC Ideas

- Implement China-Africa Cooperation in the fields of railway, highway, regional aviation networks and industrialization

- Give priority to the AU's *Programme for Infrastructure Development in Africa (PIDA)*

- Cooperate on planning and construction of infrastructural projects to achieve sub-regional connectivity and integration

we heard of an Indian narrative now coming out. India is partially opposing the whole idea of the BRI, but partially also coming up with their own grand history going back many years. So, we are hearing new voices. The BRI in the context of Africa is creating new voices, new ideas, new narratives—which is a good thing.

My third point: the BRI is primarily an infrastructural undertaking. We don't yet have political institutionalization. We have infrastructural ideas. We have corridors, but we don't yet have political institutions. So, if we talk about the Asian Infrastructure Investment Bank (AIIB), or the Silk Road Bank, these are just connected to infrastructure; they are not political ideas.

Interestingly, this idea fits perfectly into the current African need—infrastructure development. Africa wants infrastructure, going back here to the African Union's Agenda 2063 strategic framework that has also, coincidentally, been coming up. Together with the BRI, Africa wants a good infrastructure connection, a good internal interconnectivity. So, the idea of the BRI coming from China is perfectly fitting into the idea—actually happening or being discussed—within the African continent.

On the right side of the map you will see different corridors within Africa, which have been at various times conceived of by various players and have been thought through to some extent as very important corridors. The question remains: who is going to finance all these corridors?

**Lyndon LaRouche:** (interrupting from the audience): It ought to be done! What happens is, in the process of the…. [audio loss] on the development of the new [inaud] system for them. First of all, this goes way beyond anything which mankind, in Russia or elsewhere, has seen. They have no knowledge of this as such. They have now achieved, together with other people, the development of what is really a work system.

**Demissie:** Are you referring to the BRI?

## China's (new) approach towards Africa

*Goal*: industrial and agricultural cooperation

*Precondition*: **infrastructural** and human resources development

→ Growing corridorization of China's approach towards African countries

→ Not single countries but corridors becoming more important

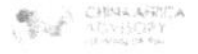

## African corridors

- Corridors as a key development tool on continental, regional and national level
- Corridors by definition link different territories or areas together
- Development & economic corridors linked to other strategic interests, such as agriculture & industrialization

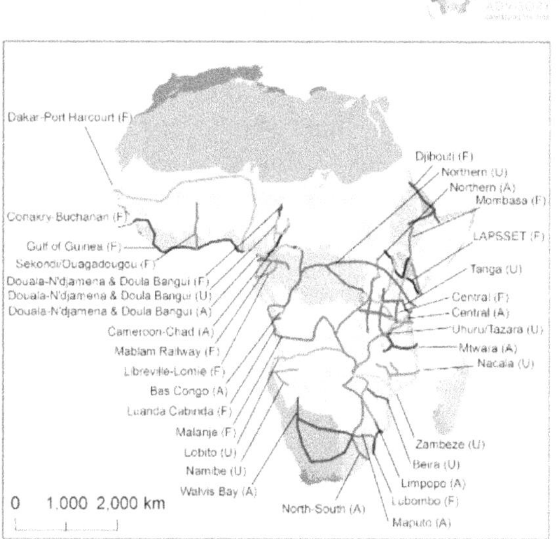


**LaRouche:** The system itself. The thing is essentially motivated by what the population has developed, what it's opened up on.

**Demissie:** Yes, yes.

**LaRouche:** Then people come in and they do some work. By this time, their mind is way beyond anything they've done before, in terms of an ongoing project. So, the job is: DO IT!

**Demissie:** Yes! Yes! Exactly! I'm fully with you on this. Because if you have been following the debate within Africa, or the African continent, or African institutions, the Agenda 2063, what we call "The Africa We Want," is nothing else than, literally, infrastructure development that the continent has been needing for decades actually, but has never happened.

We see now China as an actor coming in and literally taking up or doing part of those needed works. From the African perspective, this is a huge plus for many African countries. The idea of the BRI, coming only since 2013, is helping what has been taking place on the continent between China and the African countries since the year 2000, what we call the Forum on China-Africa Cooperation (FOCAC). For those who are not familiar with that forum, it is similar to the 16+1, where we have at least 48 African countries on the one side, with China on the other. Within this forum, the Chinese position has been always, not changing, but always adapting to the current needs.

**Lyndon LaRouche:** You *have* to change… [inaudible]

**Demissie:** Yes. I will come to that point. It has changed. I will explain how it has changed. What I meant is that it is happening every three years. Every three years this forum has been adapting, gradually, in my view, to the needs of China, actually, not only to the needs of Africa.

Since the FOCAC Summit and 6th Ministerial Conference in 2015 in Johannesburg, China has been entirely moving its priority from social-related aspects, more to hard infrastructure development aspects. China has clearly declared that they would like to see China-Africa cooperation moving into development of highways, regional aviation networks, or industrialization.

Also China has given a high priority to the African Union's program for infrastructure development. This program has approximately 51 different programs, which has translated into 400 different physical projects. I'm speaking about ports, streets, telecommunications lines—whatever is required for a nation or a continent to function.

China has also been very clear since Johannesburg in 2015 that they want to cooperate more with Africa more on infrastructural projects that create regional connectivity. That is where the BRI comes in. That's why I mentioned earlier that the BRI is primarily an infrastructure topic.

Now maybe I'm putting that emphasis here. China has also been changing its emphasis since at least 2016, clearly articulating their desire to have with Africa a cooperation on industrial and agricultural development.

Again, a physical-oriented approach. The preconditions for a developing Africa are good infrastructures in place. Good infrastructures first, and then the human resources development needs to take place at the same time.

What we see in Africa since at least two years, is a growing "corridorization" in the China-Africa relationship. By corridorization, I don't mean that single countries are no longer important, but entire regions are becoming more important for China. This is a huge departure from the bi-lateral single-country-based approach toward corridor development. If you look at the African corridors, the map on the right, you can see right now, as we speak today, around 33 different corridors that have either been developed, are under development, or are thought out and need to be developed. Corridors do nothing else but combine two different areas, and by doing so, create a development initiative, a development paradigm.

China is a big player in the corridorization movement happening in Africa, the same as we have heard about earlier with Bulgaria. You also have the same type of development going on in the Central Asian countries. The BRI is supporting these existing ideas within Africa.

From the African perspective, the questions directed to China, at least from some sub-regions, are "Is our relation to China helping us to advance those infrastructure developments we are planning? Is regional interconnectivity happening with our relationship with China? And, is the industrialization process actually happening through this relationship?

**LaRouche:** It's all are the same thing. They are not separate things.

**Demissie:** No, it's not.

**LaRouche:** You have to have these characteristics there acting, when those characteristics are coming into play. For example, I know some members of the talent there. We've worked on this. I've worked on it, in part, with my wife. The idea lying in the minds of the scientists in there, you see that the whole thing emerges in that way. The danger is that people begin to monkey around with interpretations of how this thing came about. Right now, in a short period of time, this operation has really exploded.

**Demissie:** True.

**East Africa: Leading the corridor build-up**

◆ LAPSSET
◆ SGR
◆ Djibouti-Addis Ababa railway
◆ Port Djibouti
◆ Bagamoyo
◆ Transmission lines
◆ Oil/gas pipelines
◆ Special economic zones
◆ Telecommunication

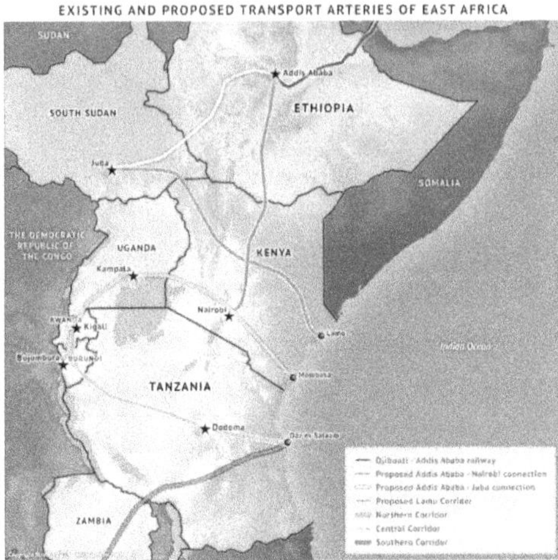



**LaRouche:** It has exploded through other groups of people. There is a connection, a very important connection of relevance, not precise. You have to work on that issue, because you have to integrate what has been the modality that you get usually. You have to work it over, change it. You have to build it up, make it stronger, reinforce it. That what the [inaud] part is. There's no magic in this thing, as such. What there is, is a hot potato, which has been ready to cook for a long period of time.

**Demissie:** I agree. But now China is coming in and is starting to cook that potato. That's actually the whole story. [laughter] It's true! We need to ask ourselves, "Why has this potato that has been lying around for ages, not been cooked until today?" In a few minutes, I'll come to the point: who is actually losing out in this "power game." I call it a power game. I'm just giving you a kind of introduction, and hopefully I'll stay within my time limit.

**East Africa**

Let's go one step lower, to East Africa. This is Africa (TIS) has been around for a long, long time. Its plans at least have been "in the drawer" for a long, long time. We know also that a lot of American research institutes played a very good role in creating those plans in the 1950s-60s, especially in Ethiopia. The Grand Renaissance Dam that is being built now on the Blue Nile in Ethiopia goes back to American scientists who created such ideas in the 1960s. A lot of ideas in East Africa, for example, have been on the table for decades, but no one was able or willing to pay for them. But now a lot of money is coming out of China, so these infrastructure projects can be built. This is actually the whole game-changing idea here about the BRI, when we bring Africa into the picture.

What is happening in East Africa? In East Africa we have different types of corridors that are shaping up, which will have a lot of effect on the livelihood of the people. There is the Lamu Port-South Sudan-Ethiopia Transport (LAPSSET) Corridor. The yellow and red, starting from here (Lamu Port) goes up to Nairobi, the capital and largest city in Kenya; up to Juba, the capital and largest city of South Sudan; then to Addis Ababa, the capital and largest city in Ethiopia; and then later to Djibouti, the capital of Djibouti.

A lot of Chinese companies are active in the Lamu Port development, and also in the new standard gauge railway (SGR) that now connects Kenya's port of Mombasa with Nairobi, inaugurated two months ago. It's functioning. It's happening. People can use those trains to go from A to B.

The same is happening now from the Djibouti port to Addis Ababa. These physical infrastructures are now in place. Their idea has always been around, but they are now in place. So, they are effectively there.

How this has changed the lives of the people is easily described. Transportation of cargo from the Djibouti port to Addis Ababa used to take three days. By train, it's now only 10 hours. Now we can imagine the economic activity will happen as a result of this single corridor development, or one infrastructure within this corridor. Yesterday, Mehreteab Mulugeta Haile, the Ethiopian General Consul spoke here about some aspects of this.

Looking at other development corridors: In Tanzania, there is the Port of Bagamoyo, approved only two weeks ago, being built with a consortium of Chinese actors with funding by Kuwait. When completed, it will be the largest port in East Africa.

The reason I mention these big projects is just to show you the kind of change they can bring into the entire region, not only to the port, but to the hinterlands behind the port. Here, again, Chinese actors are really at the forefront, changing the narrative within the African countries.

East Africa is for me the main entry point into Africa, when it comes to the BRI. I know that Egypt and

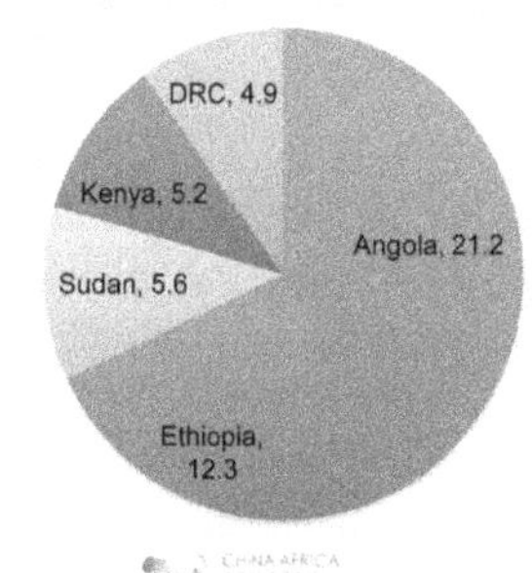

**Chinese loans to African countries**

Top 5 recipient of Chinese loans in Africa 2000-14, bn $



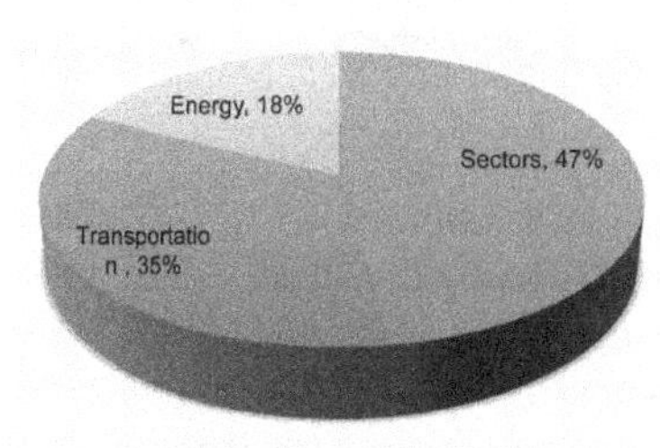

Which sectors receive the loans?



## Ethiopia: A demonstration country: Transport and Industry

Ethiopia's planned rail system

Morocco have also a big stake in the BRI, but looking at the entire development of the BRI, I consider that the East African region, starting from Djibouti in the north, down to Mozambique, will have a bigger impact on how the BRI will be coming into the African continent.

The reason why the Chinese attitude towards the African countries is also changing, is easily explained. Since 2016, China has grouped some African countries according to two classifications: "industrial cooperation demonstration and pioneering countries," that includes Tanzania, Kenya, Republic of Congo, and Ethiopia; and "priority partners for production capacity cooperation countries," that includes Egypt, Angola, and Mozambique. Very interesting wording. The point here, is that these countries will become primus inter pares; they will become a bit better than the others.

We observe the emergence of a two-phase China-Africa relationship. I might get some objection to this from my Chinese colleagues, but that's what we are observing from within Africa. We don't have the kind of big forum where every country is equal. We don't have

## Special Economic Zones

- SEZ act as "places of exception" along the infrastructural corridors
- important "attraction nodes" for Chinese companies following BRI promises into the African Region

- Supporting China's relocation strategy towards Africa

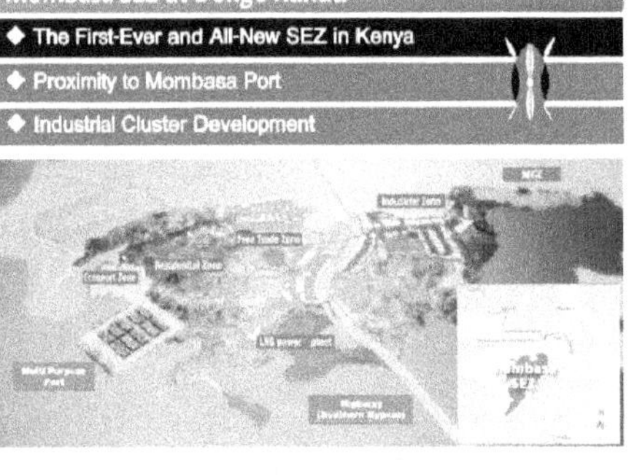


any differentiation taking place, because of those corridorizations and the BRI entry points.

Another idea I want to give you: Where is all the Chinese money? One of the questions today was "Where do the Chinese get all their money?" That's one question. But where is the money going that flows to Africa? To which sectors? Data from 2016 shows that most of the money goes to transportation and energy. Transportation is a big receiver of money from China. It encompasses trains, roads, ports, etc. This is a hint for you of where the story goes.

If we go to East Africa, we see that Ethiopia is receiving a lot of money from China, and Ethiopia is putting this money into productive sectors. They are building dams, streets, industrial parks. These are all preconditions that are required to grow faster and farther. If you don't put the money you receive (from any source) into your productive sector, then probably you will not fly very far.

Looking then at Ethiopia, shown here is the planned train connectivities within the country. Ethiopia is planning on different train routes, one of which I just mentioned, from Djibouti to Addis Ababa, has already been constructed. But there are in total eight different routes to be constructed at some point that are planned by the government. There are others in the system, such as Turkish actors, and also interest from Indian actors, but predominantly these systems will be built by Chinese enterprises.

At the same time, if you see these routes, you'll see also the proliferation of industrial zones, industrial parks within Ethiopia, all of which are being built along those train routes: infrastructural corridors. At the end, we will have "production corridors" going between various countries—Djibouti-Ethiopia, Ethiopia-Kenya, Kenya-Tanzania—so that the entire sub-region hopefully will be industrialized at some point.

Ethiopia has 22 separate industrial parks that are either planned, built, or under construction. Most are built by Chinese state-owned enterprises. This is the main point here. Special Economic Zones (SEZ) and industrial parks exist not only in Ethiopia, but are also in Kenya and Tanzania. Other countries such as Rwanda or even Senegal are following in these footsteps. They are becoming important "attraction-nauts." That's how I call them, attraction-nauts within the BRI for Chinese companies that want to go out to African countries. Without those industrial parks, there would not be so many Chinese companies in Africa.

Another area which I want to quickly show you, concerns energy production. Who is building the energy for African countries? Again, we see a lot of involvement by Chinese companies. East Africa is predominantly active in this area. "Energy" consists of anything from power plants, renewables, dams, etc. East Africa is really hard at work here. In the distribution of Chinese projects and power capacity, by sub-region until 2020, you can see that southern and eastern Africa has received quite a number of these projects.

What is the impact for African countries? Chinese actions are increasingly controlling the East African corridor development. This is one takeaway we need to make. They are working on the design, the implementation, and the financing, so the entire supply chain is controlled by Chinese actors. What I call the "infrastructure-industrial complex" is creating for African countries a very interesting mix. First, it is creating jobs. A lot of people now are getting work because of these development projects. But at the same time we see the first signs of dependency coming up. It is really important to know this. We also observe a new relation forming between increasingly powerful Chinese companies and African states. So, how do we manage those into action? Here, I'm talking about industrial capital accumulations. We heard earlier that the money that comes from China is put into the productive sectors; its not speculation money, but money that has a long time horizon, that can stay a long time in Africa. Actually, the only source currently that can have this kind of time horizon. This is distinctly different from the fast-paced speculative money coming from western countries.

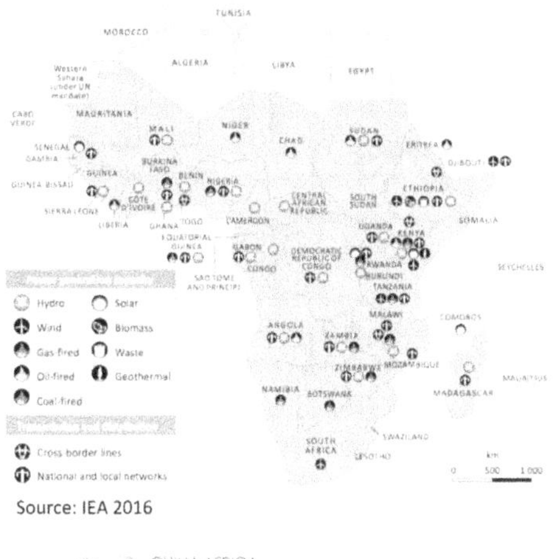

Greenfield power project contracted to Chinese companies 2010-2020

Source: IEA 2016

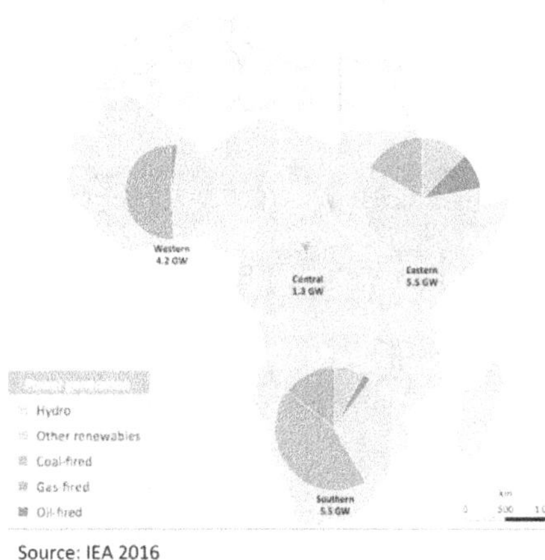

Distribution of Chinese projects in power capacity by sub-region 2010-2020

Source: IEA 2016

New market-allocation mechanisms increasingly are making it difficult for companies from the traditional partner countries to even enter the market. Even when they want to compete, they cannot compete anymore, because they are excluded from the markets. They cannot beat the competition, based on prices. So what happens when you don't even have a chance to enter the market? We see this development happening in the telecom sector and with the buildup of other infrastructure. For example, all the dam-building process in Africa right now is taking place only through Chinese enterprises. There are no other specialized players here.

China's money which is coming into African countries is not only creating industrial capital accumulations, but another "contradiction," or question for African countries: "How do you organize the labor power of people when you employ them; and how do you organize your space?" So, space organization and labor vs. money coming from China. This is one aspect we need to think really hard about.

And then, the new production centers—those industrial zones I mentioned earlier—are also creating a new interaction against traditional partners, traditional trade regimes. They are being questioned. Which is good. With the term "traditional partners," I'm referring actually directly to European actors. [laughs] Traditional development trade partners are increasingly losing out to new forms of manufacturing, capital, and location, especially coming from Asia, from China. But if China can design, finance, and implement those production centers, then that means they can also put in new rules that can exclude, easily, people they don't want. It's very easy. All this means that capital allocation will determine the kind of companies that will come in to those centers and produce.

The problem as I see it, is that the traditional partners are still in the old paradigm in their thinking. They still think with traditional assumptions: Africa is seen as an aid-dependent continent, not as a continent full of opportunities. It is still seen with the wrong mind-set. That is one of the biggest problems, and it has to change.

One question that we have been discussing recently with our Chinese colleagues is "Could a trilateral corporation—'trilateral' meaning bringing in the traditional (European) actors, Chinese actors and African actors—be a solution to this dilemma, especially for European players?" On the one hand, we can say, "Yes, it could be possible, especially if European players can use already existing Chinese-built structures, for example the special economic zones or industrial zones, to start producing in Africa as well."

We think that the traditional partners need to produce a paradigm shift in their thinking toward Africa. If they persist in thinking that Africa is just an aid-recipient continent and not a continent of opportunities, then we believe they might not have a lot of success in the coming years.

On the other hand, we need also to acknowledge that China and the African countries are not necessarily *keen* in working with European partners. If there is no paradigm shift, why should they, especially if things are working fine without them.

We see, geopolitically, a big shift happening through the BRI on the African continent that is actually affecting European actors.

That what I have from my side. Thank you very much for your time. [applause]

# The System We Live in Is Not Earthbound—Future Technologies and Scientific Breakthroughs

## Transportation, Thermonuclear Fusion, International Cooperation in Space Research

JASON ROSS

# The Economic Method of LaRouche: A Non-Scalar Approach to the Value of Science and Infrastructure

*This is an edited transcript of the keynote presentation by Jason Ross for Panel IV of the Nov. 25-26 Schiller Institute conference, "Fulfilling the Dream," held at Bad Soden am Taunis, Germany.*

I'm very happy to be here today. My name is Jason Ross and I'm with the Schiller Institute in the United States. The subject of my presentation—frankly, the reason that we're here, and a major reason that we have a new paradigm in the world right now—is the economic discoveries and method of Lyndon LaRouche, who we are very happy to have with us today. [applause]

My presentation is a three-part discussion: First, I'll

*Jason Ross*

go over some general economic concepts from LaRouche. Then I'll take up a specific case study of the economic history of a chemical element you've probably heard of, but whose uses may surprise you. And, I'll conclude with the application of LaRouche's approach to the present world situation.

## 1. General Principles

Only human beings have economies. This is a very basic concept. Only human beings have a resonance between the way our minds work—between the way we create ideas—and the way the universe works, such that our ideas have a power in the universe in a way similar to the power of electro-magnetism, or something like that, except far more powerful. That's something that is unique about human beings. Economic progress, a phenomenon unique to the human species among all known life, occurs solely by means of the discovery and social implementation of universal physical principles. This creative capability is the ultimate source of all economic growth, and of a durable basis for cooperation among peoples.

Unfortunately, economists, by and large, don't think this way. Here is a bit of evidence for what I say. This graphic (top right) shows that economists are probably *the* most failed profession on the planet, the biggest failure, absolutely biggest failure. [applause]

Take a look. In 2007, in a survey of economists in the United States, they were all asked to predict the GDP growth that they expected in 2008. As you can see from the numbers here in the histogram, the peak is about 2-3%. Most economists said there would be a 2-3% growth in GDP in 2008. Three percent of economists said that maybe there'd be a decline. They said that there was a less than 0.2% chance of a drop of GDP in excess of 2%.

What happened in 2007-8? And why did economists only give a one-in-five hundred chance of something like that occurring? This is a failure, a *dramatic* failure. It means that the basis of economic thinking is *completely* off, for the most part. Why?

The Human Population Growth chart (on the right) is from Nate Silver, *The Signal and the Noise*, based on data from the Survey of Professional Forecasters, Nov. 13, 2007.

## Population

To answer that question let's instead take a successful approach, and look at some of the metrics that Lyndon LaRouche has used. First off, let's take a long-term look at human economy, instead of just one business cycle, or "the market" this year. Let's look over thousands of years. Let's consider the historical time of the human species (on the right).

Again, we see this characteristic: that only humanity increases its population. Some of you may have heard the nostrum that "the world is overpopulated." Has anybody here heard that we have a "population problem?" Yeah. Sometimes we hear that "Africa is overpopulated." Has anybody heard that one? It's not

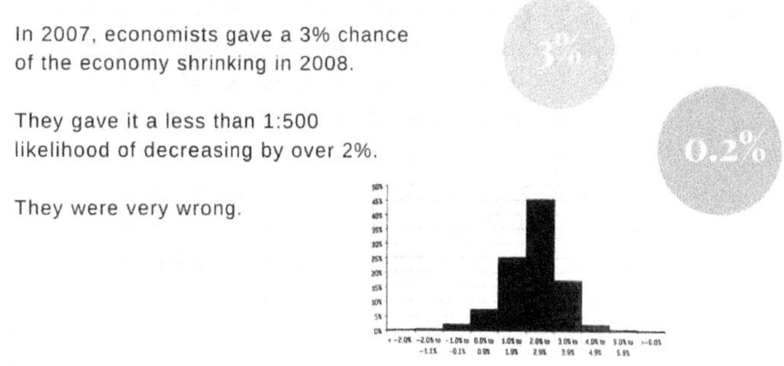



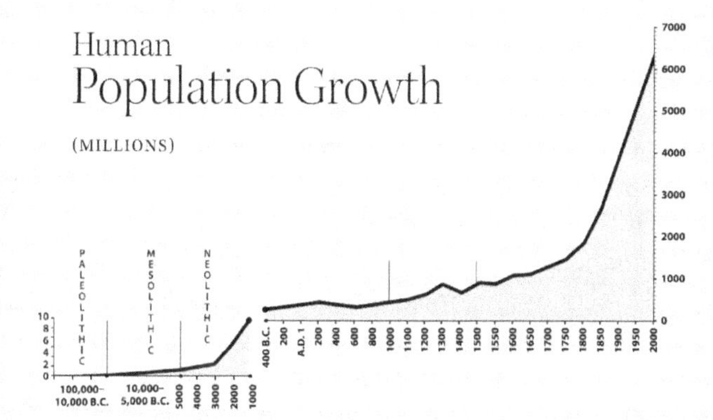



true!

We do not have a population limit! Animals have a population limit. In a hectare of land, there's a limit for the number of rabbits. For human beings, we *change* this limit. We change the *potential* human population, because we discover how nature works, and change our relationship to the surrounding nature and to each other. It's pretty simple: we are not animals!

The first basic metric that LaRouche uses in his economics textbook, is **potential relative population density**. "Population density" is an easy concept to understand: how many people live per hectare, *relative* to the quality of the land, relative to the infrastructure we've built. What's the *potential*, however? How many people *could* live in that area? What economic processes increase that number? Does the stock market increase that number? If you make money gambling on Wall Street or in the City of London, has the result of that meant that more people can live a more comfortable life on the planet? Of course not!

So, what's the source of real economic growth? A very good way to look at it is the story of Prometheus.

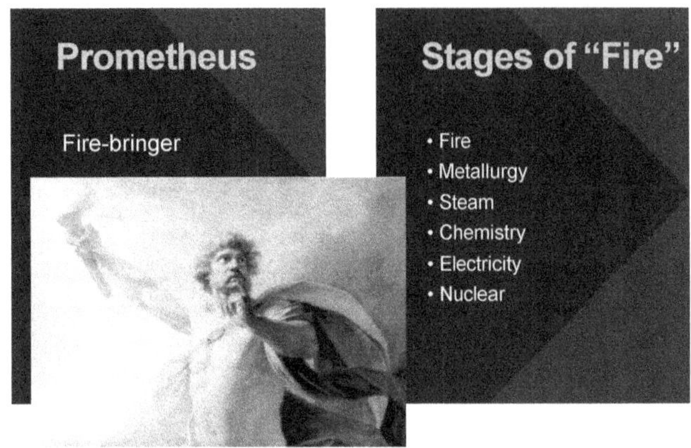


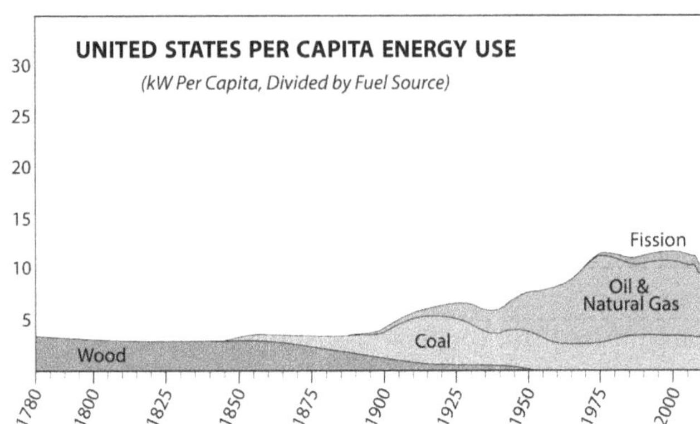


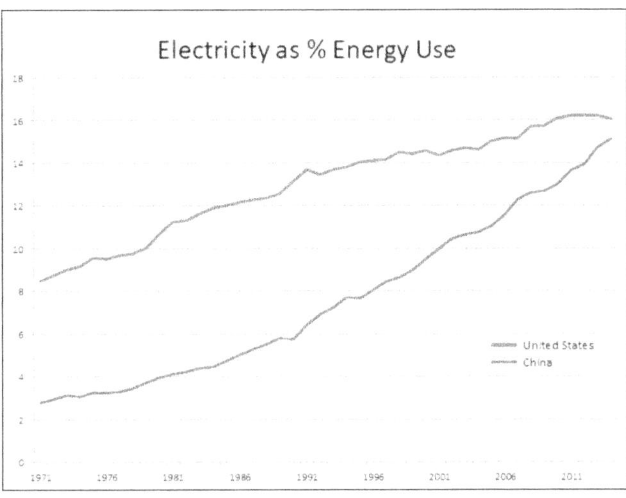


## Fire

The tale of Prometheus is a Greek story about the creation of the human species. According to this story, Prometheus gives fire to human beings, who, prior to this gift, were essentially animals. We are told by Aeschylus (BC 523-456) that Prometheus created the human species as the human species, as the creative species, the beautiful species, endowed with reason. It was Prometheus who introduced us to the use of animals and agriculture, metallurgy, the calendar, language and poetry and music, astronomy, sailing ships and navigation by the stars. But the number one gift of Prometheus was fire. Our use of fire distinguishes us from the animals. If we look at the history of the human species, perhaps from cave paintings, we find depicted there musical instruments. But the earliest evidence we have of man is fire. Wherever there were humans, there we find evidence of the use of fire.

"Fire" has changed over time. First there was only wood fire. With it we can cook our food. Think about what constitutes a resource in the wild, before fire. Is rice, is wheat? Do you eat wheat without cooking it? How about rice? We *create* resources. Even with simple, basic fire. With the hotter, purer charcoal we can have metallurgy. We can produce substances that never existed on the planet: such as bronze. Bronze is made by people. It doesn't exist in the crust of the Earth. Or consider steam power from fire. We can turn a rock (coal) into motion. Wow! Chemistry. Electricity. The development of nuclear power. The idea of fire, as a concept, has definitely expanded over time.

Let's take a look an example from the United States. You can see (top right) the amount of energy used per capita over the history of the United States. Notice that there are two trends that stand out: one is that, overall, the use of energy has increased. It stopped increasing around the time of the assassination of President John Kennedy and has remained stagnant since then. Why? Energy-efficient light bulbs? No, a shift away from industry. Secondly, notice that the *source* of power has changed, with new forms superseding the use of the old ones. As new forms of energy are developed, they do much more than allow an increased ability to do what was done before.

This brings us to our second concept from Lyndon LaRouche, which is that with a new power source, it is not just more efficient. We no longer use wood for energy. Coal is not only more efficient than wood, but it lets us do new things. Petroleum holds more energy than coal does in the same volume, but can be used to power internal combustion or jet engines. You cannot use coal to power an airplane, no matter how much you have of it. Powered flight would never have "gotten off the ground," literally, with coal.

Another example is in the use of electricity, compared to just energy overall. I've pulled together some numbers from the United States and China over the past 50 years: the percent of total energy used that is in the form of electricity, for the United States (in blue) and

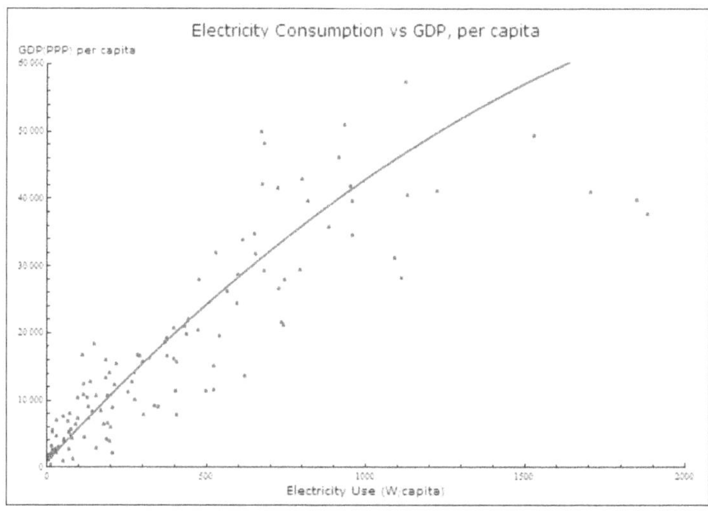



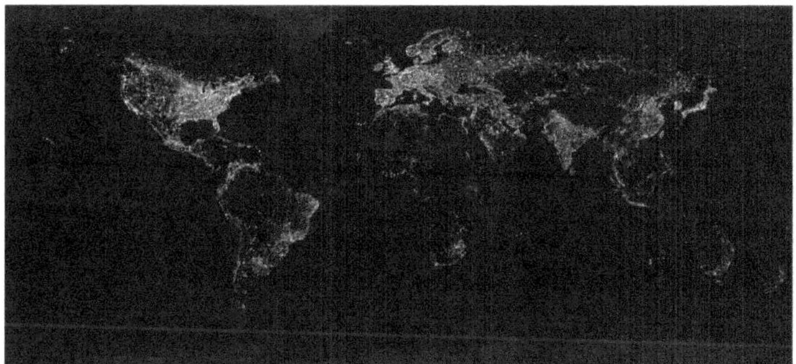

*Satellite view of earth at night.*

China (in red). You can see how it's been increasing.

Think what you can do with electricity that you couldn't do with a lower form of power. For cooking, you just need heat. For transportation and an engine, you just need heat—just explosions in an engine. What about for industry? What can you do with electricity that you can't do with a steam engine? What can you do with electricity, with a laser, with a computer-controlled machine? What can you do with translation equipment? Conference presentations? Lights? Could you have an email system powered by steam engines? Electricity is a particularly more concentrated form of energy.

This is Lyndon LaRouche's second basic metric: **energy flux density,** a measure of the concentration of energy use in the economy. We want to increase the energy used per person, but specifically, we want it to be in the most concentrated form that we can get it, because it allows us to do things that were impossible before. It's not just *"more of,"* it's *"more than."*

You can't have economic development without energy. It's central in shaping our relationship to nature and to understanding economics as a science. Here is a scatter plot (upper left). In the horizontal direction is electricity use per capita. In the vertical direction is GDP per capita (admittedly not the best measure). As you can see, it's impossible to have development without energy. I don't want to use his name, but, well—Obama's Africa Power Plan was to bring in some solar panels to put on the roof of a building here and there. Pathetic. You can't have development that way. You need the highest technology. From satellite imaging, you see this when you look at the Earth at night. The brightness of an area is actually a very good proxy for its level of development. In general, the brighter the area, the longer the lifespans of the people, the better their health, the greater their economic activity. You can see some of the dark areas, to get a sense of how differently developed different regions are.

What is the value of building an infrastructure *platform*? What is the value of having an electricity grid in a nation? Is the value of energy in a society defined by the profits of power companies? By the price paid for power? A power company might look at it in terms of how much money it gets by charging people for electricity. A rail company might ask how much money it collects in ticket fares. But, the value of energy in a society is clearly not defined by the price paid by user fees or the profits of power companies. It's not. Looking at a country as a whole, it is its infrastructure platform which reflects the level of the applied power of the minds of its citizens, and thus its economic processes.

Now turn to financing. What finance mechanisms allow us to have the overall benefit? You can see the necessity for national credit, for national banking, for example, as opposed to private investment. Private investment just can't capture the value.

## Materials

Resources. We humans change our relationship to our physical surroundings, by using the creativity of our minds to create resources. In the picture at the top of the next page, on the right you see a green rock. On the left, a tiny puddle of copper that was made from that rock. That rock is malachite. It's a very common ore that we use to make copper today. Six thousand years ago, it was used by the Egyptians to make green paint. With the coming of the Bronze Age, malachite ceased to be just a rock, and became a source of copper metal. We created this transformation.

So, what is a resource? Is this rock a resource? On

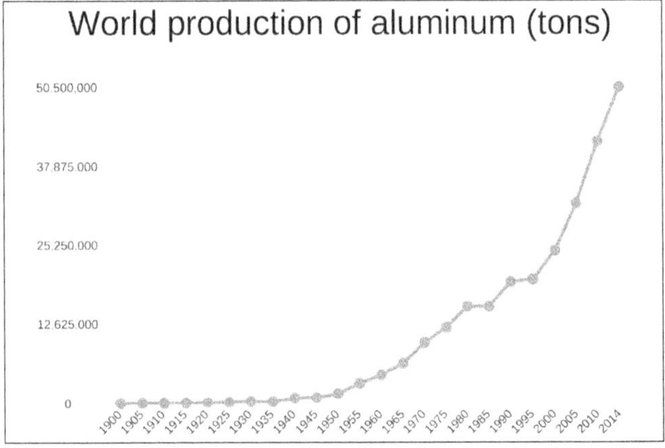

World production of aluminum (tons)



its own, it's a color. With the advent of metallurgy, that rock, combined with another rock, a source of tin, becomes a source of a new material, bronze, from which we can make better tools.

Here's another example: aluminum (chart). Before the advent of age of electricity, aluminum was very rarely used. It's very difficult to produce aluminum in a chemistry laboratory. Aluminum binds very strongly to oxygen. It doesn't want to let it go. Today, we make aluminum by the application of large amounts of electricity. As you can see, as electricity developed, the production of aluminum has skyrocketed. Nowadays (some recycling aside) we routinely throw it out, as it's no longer considered that valuable after its initial consump-

tion. That is a change in the availability of that resource, due to our development. Resources are not limited! We create new ones all the time. That's economics.

If someone should ask you about "natural resources," adding, maybe, that "we're running out of them," tell them the biggest resource we have is our minds. That is the source of *all* of our resources, except for maybe some berries that you might find out in the woods. The lesson here is that there are no truly "natural" resources. We *make* all our resources and then we use them, to better or worse effect.

**Transportation**

The scientific discoveries we make also change our relationship to space, time, and distance. Here are maps of the United States (below), showing, for different years, how fast someone could travel away from New York City. At first, on the left, you see the year 1800. The thick lines are initially numbers of days, then numbers of weeks—how many days and how many weeks it takes to reach a location away from New York City. By 1830, you could go much farther. Why? The building of roads and canals. Here's 1857. More canals, the beginnings of the railroads. By 1930 (see next page), you could reach across the whole country in just a few days. The railroad crosses the entire country. Roadways have been built. It's a *different country*. What's the value of building that rail system? What's the value of air flight? Is it the freight or passenger charges that the railroads and airlines collect? Of course not! It's a new type of economy. The transcontinental railroad and intercontinental flight annihilated distance and time, bringing a nation and nations closer together, culturally, economically, physically.

How do we represent such a transformation? Well, Lyndon LaRouche refers us to the "LaRouche-Riemann Method," pointing to the work of Bernhard Riemann's

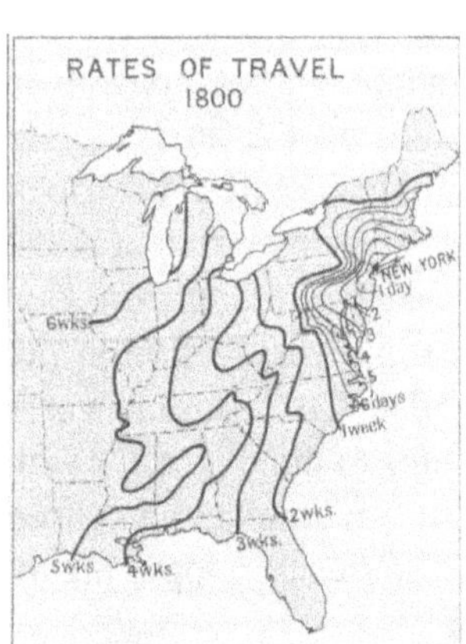


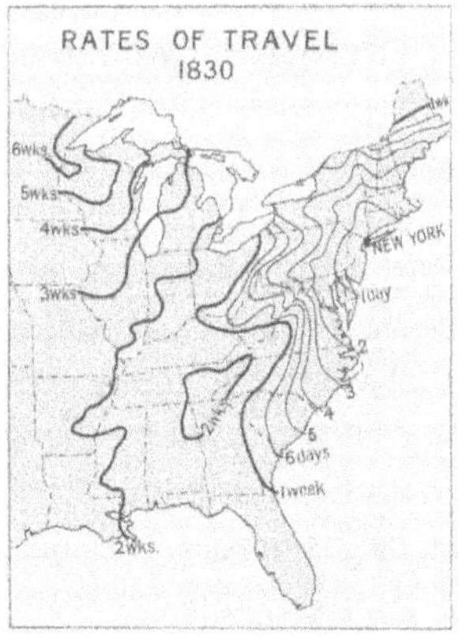


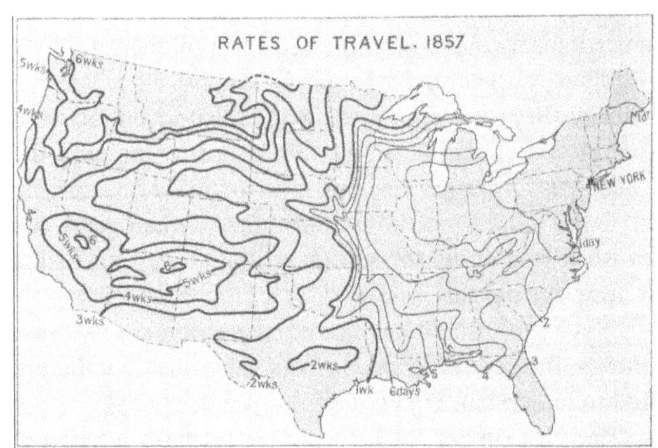

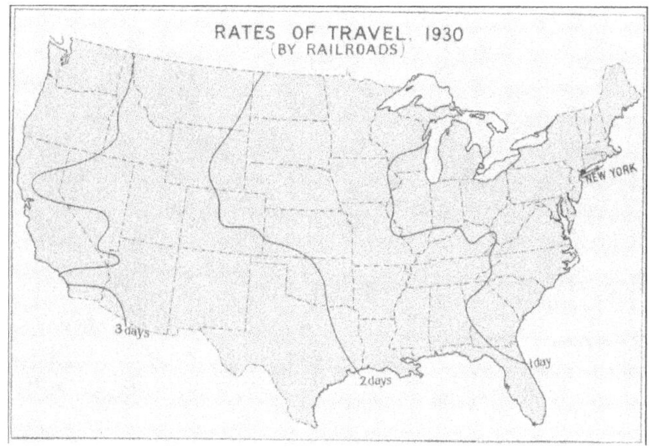



laying out a basis for understanding changes that are not only numerical, or quantitative, but you might say dimensional. Having a national rail network is almost like going from a flat, two-dimensional world to a three-dimensional one. There's a new domain of possibility for us. That new domain of action made possible by the new platform of infrastructure, or a newly discovered universal physical principle, allowing for further applications of creative thought, is *itself* the value.

Increasing the rate of increase of potential relative population density is the true location of economic value.

## 2. Case Study: Uranium

Let's now apply this understanding to a specific resource that mankind has used for a very long time: uranium. Uranium has been a human resource for at least 2,000 years. I don't know if you knew that or not. Two thousand years ago, the Romans used uranium in their glass-making, to impart a nice yellow-green color. This use, and other physical characteristics in glass-blowing, have continued for two millennia. How much of a resource is this? How important? Well, not very important. Nice, but not really a big deal. In the 1950s, uranium was used in glass in electrical components. Here's another example of uranium glass (below). That's one

thing you can do with uranium—an application of a simple *physical* property: its color and consistency.

The next big use of uranium came in the early 1900s. It played an important role in revolutionizing agriculture. One of the main components for fertilizing the soil, the nutrients that the German chemist Justus von Liebig (1803-1873) figured out that were necessary to promote healthy plant growth, is nitrogen. Nitrogen is a key component. It's the main component of fertilizers that we use today, along with potassium and other things. Where does nitrogen come from? The atmosphere all around us is 80% nitrogen. Plants can't use it directly from the air, however. For them to do so, it has to be converted, "fixed," by incorporating it into a compound, such as ammonia, nitrite, or nitrate. Lightning helps out by fixing a significant amount of nitrogen. Most fixed nitrogen is a product of bacteria living in the soil or symbiotically in the roots of legumes. Over time, farmers learned that rotating the planting of legumes—such as alfalfa, or soy—in their fields resulted in their other plants growing better. The bacteria add more nitrogen to the soil. It's a very slow process.

In the 1800s, we came up with "artificial" ways of adding nitrogen. We mined saltpeter (potassium nitrate) and applied the manure of certain animals directly to the soil. Guano—bat and bird poop—was transported all around the world from caves in such places as Chile and various islands out in the middle of the oceans, be-

*Fritz Haber (left), Albert Einstein, (right), 1914.*

cause of its value as fertilizer. But there are only so many bats and birds, so the supply is limited. Faced with growing food needs for a growing world population, how did we expand the production of nitrogen?

In the photo (previous page), you see Fritz Haber (on the left) with Albert Einstein. In 1909, Haber developed a famous process named after him, the Haber-Bosch process, a technique that was scaled up to industrial levels by BASF's Carl Bosch. (They both received Nobel Prizes for this work.) The Haber-Bosch process converts nitrogen from the air into ammonia, and thus makes it usable for plants. How does it work? One of the first catalysts used by Haber to change nitrogen's chemical bonds, was uranium. In this case, uranium's *chemical* properties were called into play, to facilitate a chemical reaction, to produce the nitrogen fertilizer to feed people. Today, the modern Haber-Bosch process no longer uses uranium, but I'll tell you an amazing statistic: an astonishing one-third of the nitrogen that is entering into the soil to be used by plants, is made by the Haber-Bosch process, and of the 2-3 kg of nitrogen in our bodies, fully 40% of that comes from the Haber-Bosch process. What an amazing change in our relationship to our environment!

That clearly increases our potential relative population density, when we can create fertilizer from the air. This is a clear economic benefit.

As our knowledge expanded, uranium's role as a human resource changed: from its physical use (appearance of glass) to its chemical use (nitrogen fertilizer) to its nuclear use (huge amounts of power). Today, the vast majority of uranium is used in nuclear power plants, to make tremendous amounts of electricity from very little fuel, by undergoing a nuclear reaction.

## Nuclear Fusion

I want to say a little bit here about why nuclear power is so excellent. Here you see two similar-looking reactions, in one case a chemical reaction, and the other a nuclear one. On the left is a molecule of methane ($CH_4$), otherwise known as natural gas, or cooking gas. It is a carbon with four hydrogens. When methane combines with oxygen in a chemical reaction, it burns to produce carbon dioxide and water, and the amount of energy released is 8 electron-volts. Don't worry for now about what an electron-volt is. For now, just remember the number is 8.

On the right, we have nuclear fusion. We have a

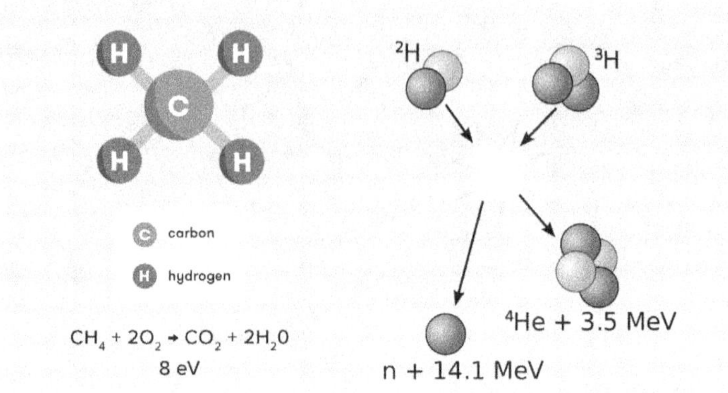



*Power output from burning of methane (left) and from a Deuterium-Tritium fusion reaction.*

combination of deuterium ($^2H$) and tritium ($^3H$), two types of hydrogen. When they combine, they make helium ($^4He$) and a neutron, and you can see the number: together, a whopping 17.6 *mega* electron-volts—two million times more energy in the nuclear reaction, compared to reactions in the chemical realm. This is why nuclear power plants need such a tiny amount of fuel. It is inherently a more powerful domain of knowledge. With our discovery of nuclear processes, we've potentially unleashed a million times more power for our use.

How can we use that power? How does that increase the potential human population density? What higher densities of energy flux processes does this allow? I'll give you an example of where it would be great if we had much more nuclear power.

In 2015, the *New Horizons* spacecraft launched by NASA passed by Pluto to study it. This is the way Pluto looked before *New Horizons,* and the way it looked after. Much better. [laughter] It took ten years for *New Horizons* to reach Pluto. It flew by in about four hours. Why didn't it stop? One reason is that it's going to go farther out to research a Kuiper Belt object. But also, it *couldn't* stop. It didn't have any fuel left in its engines. For chemical rockets, you burn up all the fuel at launch and then just coast until you get to where you're going. That's called ballistic flight. To send humans to Mars this way would take nine months with chemical-fired rockets. Maybe you've seen videos of astronauts upon their return to Earth after even relatively short missions. They can't even walk. Can you imagine going to Mars and then trying to do anything there? You wouldn't even be able to stand.

With nuclear-powered rockets, on the other hand, we will go to Mars in a week or two, rather than 9

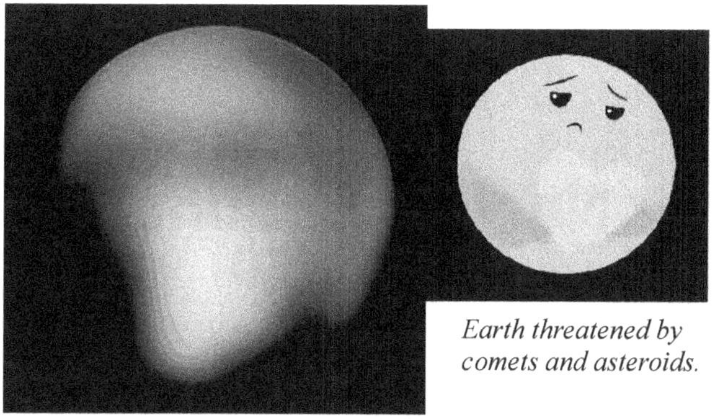

*Earth threatened by comets and asteroids.*

months. We will be able to push away incoming comets and asteroids which threaten Earth and us. And with fully developed nuclear fusion, we will totally transform our relationship to energy, to materials, to water. With such an incredible source of power, water desalination is no longer a big deal. We can do it in a massive way. This is the next stage of fire, to be reached as soon as possible. It deserves the highest of funding priorities!

## 3. Application

Over decades of work by Lyndon and Helga LaRouche and by the Schiller Institute, we've got a new paradigm that's taking over the world, and an old paradigm that needs to be brushed aside. Very importantly, we've got the specific kinds of concepts that need to be introduced into political and economic thought, to create policies for the future, which would mean, for example, a *tremendous* research effort into fusion energy. Fusion energy research in the United States today is pathetic. There are really only a couple of fusion facilities. The other two have been shut down, or are under reconstruction. It's pathetic. If you think about how much money is spent researching better wind turbines and better solar panels to try to coax out *slightly* more energy from sunshine while neglecting fusion which would be an *immense* source of power, it's completely insane. That would be one of the key trajectories to launch into: international cooperation to bring the next platform of economic development to the world.

As my colleague Hussein Askary showed us yesterday, the greatest population growth on the planet in the future will be in Africa and Southwest Asia. The potential for economic growth in these regions is unparalleled, with the greatest potentials for gains to be accomplished by leapfrogging to the highest available technologies, and by applying mental resources to developing the great discoveries of the future. It is possible to speak of the economic value of culture, of our understanding of ourselves our relationships to each other, and the almost miraculous capability of the mind to develop thoughts that have the power to reshape the universe. The question posed by this ability remains: "What is God, that Man is in His image, that Man's thoughts resonate with universal causes?"

The human mind is the ultimate resource, and it need never be exhausted. This is the proper starting point for economic science.

Thank you for your attention! [applause]

**The World Land-Bridge Network—Key Links and Corridors**
*Committed, underway or completed.

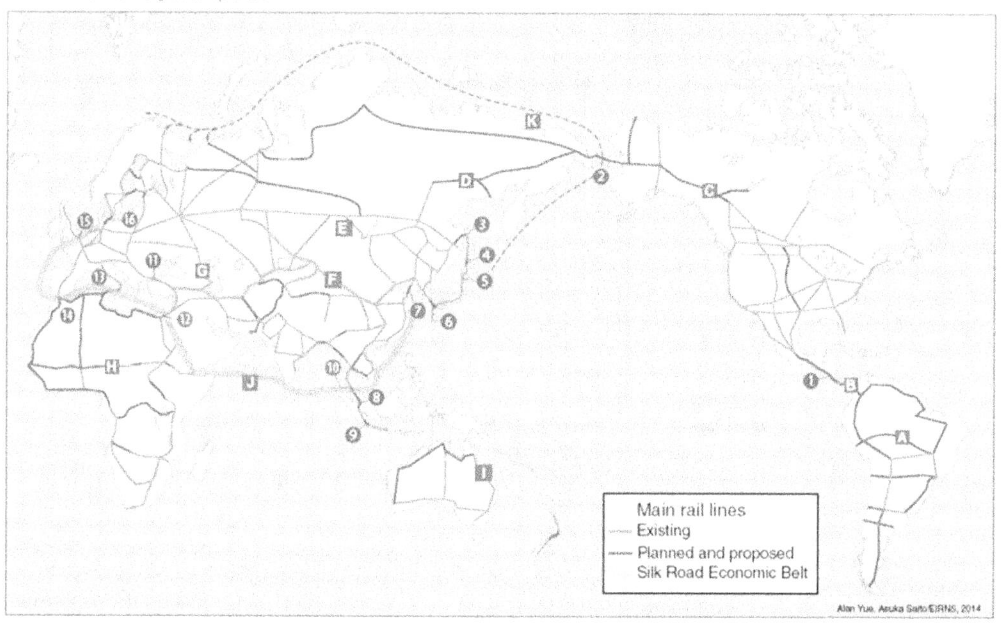

# The System We Live in Is Not Earthbound

*The following are summary reports of the presentations of Guo Wentao and Professor Dr. Helmut Alt, and the discussion following the panel on Nov. 26, day two of the Schiller Institute Conference, "Fulfilling the Dream of Mankind." The Panel focused on Future Technologies and Scientific Breakthroughs (Transportation, Thermonuclear Fusion, International Cooperation in Space Research).*

## GUO WENTAO
## Current Situation of High Temperature Gas-Cooled Reactor in China

*Guo Wentao is from the Paul Scherrer Institute, the largest research institute for natural and engineering sciences in Switzerland.*

Guo Wentao spoke about one of the most advanced designs for nuclear power production: the high-temperature gas-cooled reactor. First developed in the 1960s by Rudolf Schulten, the reactor has numerous safety fea-

*Wentao Guo*

tures which make it meltdown-proof. The reactor is based on a simple design which can facilitate low-cost, speedy construction, and a very convenient form for the use of fuel. In this design, fuel "pellets," each one comprising a uranium core with a heat-resistant and distance-maintaining coating, are introduced into the reactor from the top and removed from the bottom. Once removed, the pellets are tested, and will then be either reintroduced into the top to serve as fuel again, or sent to storage. Reprocessing of the pellets is also a possibility.

China currently has one such reactor, the HTR-10 test facility in Beijing. A 1,000 MW design is currently in the final stages of construction and fuel assembly in Shidao Bay. Interest in the Chinese design has been expressed by several nations, including Saudi Arabia. Guo expressed his happiness with the portion of the conference he was able to attend, and

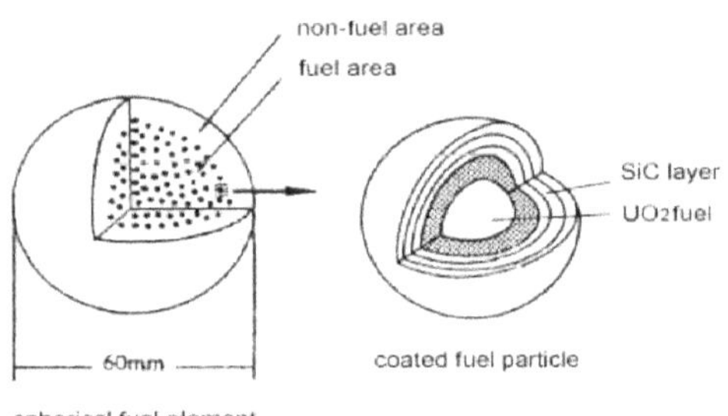


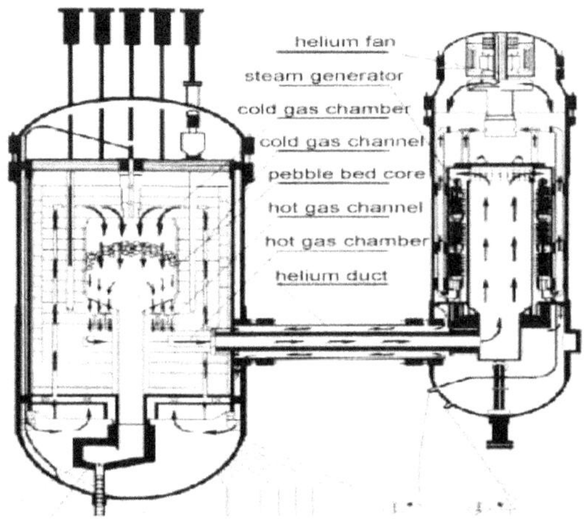

was glad to meet a group that supported nuclear power. He presented to the conference audience a clear idea of the highest currently available form of power, and on China's rapid commercial development of the technology.

## DR. HELMUT ALT
## Energy Transition—from Bad to Worse

*Helmut Alt*

*Professor Dr. Helmut Alt is from the University of Applied Sciences (Fachhochschule), Aachen, Germany.*

Professor Helmut Alt spoke about the devastating effects of the German decision to move backwards on the scale of energy, with the *Energiewende* policy of shutting down nuclear power and ramping up investment in wind and solar. He reminded the audience that in the modern world, life without electricity is simply impossible and pointed out the fact that the devastating tidal wave that struck Japan and killed tens of thousands, also caused a problem with the Fukushima nuclear plant, but unlike the tidal wave, the problem with the nuclear plant did not result in mass deaths. Professor Alt focused on prevailing myths about energy: that nuclear power receives large subsidies (current renewable subsidies in Germany are over 20 times the peak nuclear subsidy, which was over two decades ago); that solar and wind are a useful addition to the energy supply (Germany routinely pays millions of dollars per sunny and windy day to give away excess electricity produced by these sources, which typically produce far less than is needed); and that German reductions of $CO_2$ could have any meaningful impact on global climate.

Dr. Alt presented, in brief, the German history of nuclear development, from Lise Meitner and Otto Hahn, to the German record of routinely having at least 8 of the top 10 nuclear plants in the world. Germany, now, has committed itself to closing all of its nuclear plants by 2022. As a result of this policy, enormous subsidies and extra costs have driven up power bills to around 300% of their year 2000 levels for both homes and for industry. After an extensive and humorous demonstration of the numerous absurd results of German energy policy, Alt concluded that these decisions, reached by the democratic process, require a significant campaign of education to resolve.

# Panel IV Discussion

The first question built upon a theme introduced by Hussein Askary in Panel II, on the myth of the Chinese land grab in Africa. Dr. Alexander Demissie, who had spoken on Panel III, responded by refuting the false reporting and by laying out the positive role of Chinese involvement in improving African agriculture. This contrasts with the actual land grabs taking place in Asia—pointed out by Askary—by Europeans taking land out of food production and moving it to biofuels.

The next question concerned popular fears of nuclear "waste" as a huge cost for future generations. Professor Alt addressed the well-known technical feasibility of storing spent nuclear fuel, in such locations as salt mines. The problems have never been technically insurmountable, but rather have been sabotaged politically.

Further questions concerned new fields of science and technology, and the economic inferences drawn from the image of the world at night. The shortfall of electricity supply in Africa is astounding. Sub-Saharan Africa averages 45 watts per capita, with the Democratic Republic of Congo, for example, as low as 20. This is despite the DRC being the location of the planned Grand Inga Dam complex, which will produce 40,000 MW of electricity, enough for 100 million people at a medium development level. World Bank participation in this hydroelectric wonder, part of the African Union's vision for the continent in 2063, was terminated in 2016 for supposedly "environmental" reasons.

# Schiller Institute November 25-26 Conference

Helga Zepp-LaRouche proposed two resolutions at the Schiller Institute Conference in Bad Soden titled *Fulfilling the Dream of Mankind*. Both resolutions passed unanimously.

## Europe Must End Poverty for Its 120 Million Poor by 2020

At this conference, with the title *Fulfilling the Dream of Mankind*, we discussed the incredible transformation of the world catalyzed by the Chinese initiative of the New Silk Road. The Belt and Road Initiative, which is creating optimism in Asia, Africa, Latin America, more and more states in Europe, and after the state visit of President Trump in China, in several states within the United States.

The Belt and Road Initiative has a concrete perspective for overcoming poverty and underdevelopment through investment in infrastructure, industry, and agriculture, based on scientific and technological progress. The Chinese government, which lifted 700 million people out of poverty in the last 30 years, has now proclaimed the goal to lift the remaining 42 million living in poverty out of their condition, and to create a decent living standard for the entire Chinese population by the year 2020.

Within the European Union, there are approximately 120 million people below the poverty line, according to our own criteria characterizing the costs of life. Given the fact that Europe is still an economic powerhouse, there is no plausible reason why Europe cannot lift these 120 million people out of poverty by the year 2020, as well. The best way to accomplish this is for the EU, for all European nations to accept the offer from China to cooperate with China in the Belt and Road Initiative on a "win-win" basis.

We, the participants of the Schiller Institute conference, call on all elected officials to join this appeal to the European governments. Should we in Europe not be proud enough to say, if the Chinese can do this, we can do it, too?

## The War and Humanitarian Crisis in Yemen

Given the documented fact that the war on Yemen, waged by the Saudi-led coalition since March 2015, has caused an unprecedented humanitarian crisis in this country as a result of the bombardment of the country's infrastructure and the total blockade imposed by air, land and sea, the attendees of the Nov. 25-26, 2017 Schiller Institute international conference in Bad Soden, Germany call for:

1. An immediate ceasefire by all parties;

2. The lifting of the blockades imposed on the country, especially the port of Hodeida and the Sana'a International Airport, allowing in immediate humanitarian aid;

3. The return to the national reconciliation process and dialogue that was underway, but was interrupted by the war. (This negotiation process needs to be conducted under the UN umbrella, by only Yemeni national factions, without interference from regional or global powers, but with the sponsorship of Russia, China, and the United States as guarantors of the implementation of the final outcome of the dialogue.) The purpose of such negotiations is to find a political solution to the crisis in Yemen.

4. Assisting Yemen in a rapid and large-scale reconstruction process focused on infrastructure projects to regain the livelihood of the nation, and the integration of Yemen into the Belt and Road Initiative.

# What Is a Nation? Nations as Dynamical[1]

---

*The global crisis which the just-inaugurated Presidency of Barack Obama has inherited, involves profoundly elementary forms of existential challenges for each and all peoples of the planet, challenges of a type which are beyond anything which recent governments of any part of the world have been willing to face heretofore. The rescue of those governments and their putative experts, demands some profound, and also shocking changes from the conceptions which have, heretofore, misguided the leading professionals involved in advising the most relevant leading governments of various regions of the world.[2]*

*My recent, extraordinary success of July 25, 2007, in long-range economic forecasting of crucial developments in the world's economic systems, should have become, by now, sufficient, even virtually overwhelming evidence of the need to abandon what had been, heretofore, the leading assumptions respecting economy by governments and others, and to adopt new, more appropriate principles which would be consistent with the validated methods of forecasting employed by me.[3] That forecast has become a breakthrough, toward a sweeping, fundamental change in the future meaning of the very name of economics, sweeping aside everything which had been considered professional expertise up to the point of that most recent development.*

*However, now that the inauguration has occurred, the new President and his Presidency, for their part, are now justly occupied, for the moment, with the proverbial "bits and pieces" of maintaining their "tempo of control" over the day-to-day role of the President in establishing and maintaining his office's control over its function of moment-to-moment national and world leadership in the current, virtually unprecedented crisis in the national and world situations. This compels that President to resort to large doses of improvisation; for, if he were to lose control, hostile foreign as well as domestic forces will be able to act to immobilize the Presidency's ability to exert management control over the current situation.*

*In the meantime, circles and individuals associated with the institution of the Presidency, whether formally attached to it, or implicitly committed to its success, must generate programs and perceptions which are of a more long-range, lasting significance for the history of the republic and the world. Thus, while the new Administration is preoccupied with what may be characterized as "swatting flies," solid, long-ranging measures must be crafted and put into place for the long haul— soon. In the end, as the months pass, it will be those long-haul effects which will be crucial for this present Administration. This report of mine is focused on those conceptions which represent the most important among those urgent "long haul," elements of policy.*

*The most crucial, and also least understood, among those still controversial conceptions on which the survival of civilization on this planet now depends, is the issue of principle which I present in this report:*

*So, in remarks which I had delivered to a leadership meeting of January 13th, I emphasized the following:*

---

1. This report was prepared in response to an important question, presented by relevant professionals, presented to me during the Question & Answer period of the January 22, 2009 LaRouche PAC webcast.

2. From misleading conceptions premised upon the notion of money, to that of physical values.

3. Learn the homely wisdom of the ghosts in the celebrated German film ***Spukschloss im Spessart*** who said, *"Die Hauptsache ist der Effekt"* ("The effect is what's most important").

*1.) That, the systemic distinction, both physical and moral, between a species of animal life and a sovereign individual member of a human culture, is a difference expressed, in the human individual, as a process of development of* an implicitly immortal, subsuming principle, *a principle whose expression occurs within an individual of a specific generation, but, a principle which, nonetheless, subsumes, ontologically, the way in which the ultimate outcome of* a succession of generations *of a nation is actually, intentionally ordered for effect.*

*For societies which are capable of surviving this present world crisis, we have now reached the point that, no more can anyone who wishes to be considered competent, tolerate the assumption, that the process of an economy should be treated as being contained in a way in accord with the dogma of the unfortunate René Descartes: that as if within what were to be treated as merely a reflection of the externally influenced, mechanical-like interactions of the inanimate, or mortal individual subjects as such.*

*2.) What I was emphasizing in that report to the meeting of my associates, was the following.*

*The consistent failure of most attempts at long-range economic forecasting by my putative rivals from among the sundry economists and relevant others of nations, should have warned us, that we must reject the notion, that the controlling* physical cause *of mass economic behavior could be what appears to have been a statistical succession of individual developments in society: as if embodying, as if mechanically, the physically efficient cause of the existence and behavior of each of the subsumed, presumably discrete elements of that succession.*

*For example: Contrary to mechanistic presumptions, Johannes Kepler's uniquely original discovery of an efficient universal principle of Solar gravitation, in his* **The Harmonies of the World**, *remains, in fact, today, a prime example of what Gottfried Leibniz defined, during the 1690s, as a principle of physical dynamics. The categorical point of distinction of human society from animal ecologies, is a comparable case. The same* harmonic *quality of systems, is the subject of the physical science of such as Bernhard Riemann, V.I. Vernadsky, and Albert Einstein.*

*The dynamic quality of nations is fostered through scientific and technological achievements and their introduction into the physical economy, promoting the general welfare. This Leibnizian conception was well understood by Benjamin Franklin, whose scientific exploration of electricity is portrayed here by Benjamin West.*

*The great fault of all recently prevalent assumptions governing the economic thought of professional economists and related circles, whether among the academics, or the opinion of the street gambler, lies in the influence of the axiomatic presumptions of the practice of usury, assumptions which were summed up by Adam Smith, not in his virulently anti-American tract of 1776, his* **Wealth of Nations**, *but his earlier apology for the mystical irrationality of philosophical liberalism, an apology given in what should have been considered today as his more thorough promotion of the Ockhamite Liberalism of Paolo Sarpi, as in Smith's 1759* **Theory of the Moral Sentiments**. *The exclusion of the possibility of a physical-dynamic (e.g., Leibnizian, Riemannian)*

# Kepler on Aristotle

*Johannes Kepler refuted Aristotle's geocentric cosmology, and charged that Aristotle held science back for nearly two millennia, until the advent of Copernicus, by rejecting the Pythagorean idea that the Earth moves in an orbit around the Sun. Here is an excerpt. Kepler's full document was published in* 21st Century Science & Technology, *Winter 2001-02.*

I am as little satisfied with Aristotle, when he thinks it is sufficient to have asked why the Earth remains at the center of the world, and to answer, that nature assigned this position to it. For it is entirely uncertain, and not conceded by me, that the Earth is in the middle of the world; and were it so, it would be so indeed on account of nature, but in the same way that all things are on account of nature. But one is not satisfied to know that things are according to nature, but one asks why they are that way and not some other way, and what means nature used to bring this about....

*Johannes Kepler (1571-1630)*

*basis for economic value, rather than a monetarist one, is the great error of academic and Las Vegas gambler alike, an error which must be now suddenly expelled from the practice of economy by governments, if civilization is to survive this present crisis.*

*Therefore, if civilizations wish to survive the presently onrushing, global economic breakdown-crisis, they must change their ways accordingly, shifting to the legacy of the physical science of Nicholas of Cusa, Leonardo da Vinci, Johannes Kepler, Pierre de Fermat, and Gottfried Leibniz, away from popular sentiments such as those prescribed by Paolo Sarpi follower Adam Smith's* **Theory of the Moral Sentiments**. *It is that Liberalism of the dupes of Paolo Sarpi, which also made a*

*dupe of not only Karl Marx, but many of Marx's followers, among many other types of cases of the same radically reductionist madness.*

*The distinction of the subject of this present report, is its attention to, and explanation of the fact, that that which is expressed in the manner in which the living human individual, who is mistakenly seen as merely biological, is actually shown to be the embodiment of something which is subsumed by the superior efficiency of a higher principle. That principle is one which must appear to our biologists, not as a principle of biology as they have usually defined it heretofore, but, as what must tend to appear to most literate observers as an eerie sort of spiritual principle, as that creative potential of the individual human mind which is lacking in all lower forms of life.*

*I refer, here, to the distinctive quality of a principle of human intelligence, a higher sort of principle which is expressed as original, or replicated discoveries of universal physical principles, or as artistic compositions expressing truly original and valid principles of composition. Eerie as this notion might appear to be to some persons, at first glance, it is, nonetheless, actually (ontologically) a physically efficient principle of our universe. It is to be treated as an expression of a physically efficient principle of dynamics, rather than a mere effect, for example, of such as a Cartesian-like datum of the reductionist classroom's statistical dogma.*

*Thus, in the matter of the relevance of the work of Academician Vernadsky, there are three, mutually distinct ontological qualities of such integral, dynamical systems to be considered by us here: a.) The general abiotic ("pre-life"); b.) Living processes, and their specific by-products, other than those of human mind; and, c.) The human mind. In these cases, the distinction of the higher one, is not a derivative of the nature the lower, but, rather, all three are commonly subsumed by a higher, common, universal, dynamic (creative:* anti-entropic*) principle, as Albert Einstein summed up the combined effect of the uniquely original discoveries of the Solar System's principle of gravitation of Johannes Kepler and those of Bernhard Riemann, defining our universe as a finite, but not externally bounded universe.*

*In other words, I mean dynamics as* dynamics *(the echo of Classical Greek* dynamis*) was defined by Gottfried Leibniz's attack on Descartes, on this specific account. The fuller meaning of a general principle of dynamics in modern science, was given later by Bernhard Riemann, as this is typified for today's general reference by his 1854 habilitation dissertation. Further contributions to the elaboration of Riemann's discovery have been supplied, most notably, by the anti-mechanistic discoveries of Max Planck (e.g., harmonics, rather than Ernst Mach's "mechanics"), Albert Einstein, and Academician Vernadsky.*

*3.) The principle which I have identified in the opening of this prologue, is of the same quality of form as that expressed by Johannes Kepler's uniquely original discovery of a universal principle of gravitation. So, Albert Einstein identified his own, Riemannian view of Kepler's work, as pin-pointed in Kepler's Book IV of* **The Harmonies,** *as being the enveloping foundation of* **all** competent, modern physical-science practice.[4]

*4.) So, I have emphasized, over decades to date, that in that competent way of thinking within the domain of physical science, this difference is expressed in the terms of what Gottfried Leibniz defined, in his denunciation of Descartes, as* dynamics. *As I have said above, this is a notion of dynamics which Leibniz identified as an echo of the notion called* dynamis *among the ancient Greek and related circles of the Pythagoreans and Plato. The same notion, as developed in an enriched form by Bernhard Riemann and his followers, such as Albert Einstein, is crucial for defining the functional notion of the necessary integrity of a*

*sovereign nation. Einstein's expressed, Riemannian views, insofar as they are known to me, lack only the needed, still higher standpoint of reference, to Academician V.I. Vernadsky's Riemannian notion of the Noösphere.*

*5.) The application of this conception, so summarized above, supplies modern civilization with a specific notion of nation-state cultures which is crucial in addressing the root of that grave crisis of global civilization which is presently menacing humanity as a whole, as at this present moment.*

*In these days of a world of humanity now plunging at an accelerating rate toward depths which have not been thought possible, everything on which I expend significant efforts now, has both a long-term and an immediate purpose, that in service of the defense of the immediate, terrible threat to very existence of a civilized form of life on this planet. This condition of presently accelerating, global crisis, makes demands upon me, which bear upon the unique competencies which I have developed in the field of a science of physical economy. Thus, what I must present as of urgent relevance on this account, may appear to verge on the merely academic, but no one should be misled into thinking that what I write in the following piece is "merely academic" in any meaningful sense. The following is written in what must be identified as "deadly serious" intent, and must be read accordingly.*

*That intent and character of what I write below, will be clear enough as the following account unfolds.*

---

## Introduction:
## On the Subject of One's Self

My specific contribution to the principles of dynamics being delivered within this present literary location, lies within those dynamics of humanity, as such, which underlie the actual characteristics of *physical* economies. This can be usefully illustrated, for these purposes, by a brief reference to a closely related aspect which is typical of my own, relevant personal experience, and in relatively greater, or lesser degree by some relevant others. I point out some notably relevant autobiographical items, as follows.

All but one of my grandparents were born during the 1860s, amid the setting of the decade of the great

---

4. Kepler's demonstration that neither the sense of sight, nor hearing could account for the harmonic composition of the Solar System, freed science from the grip of the folly of sense-certainty, especially the folly of the modern European empiricism of the followers of Paolo Sarpi. Although this had been anticipated by Cardinal Nicholas of Cusa, as in Cusa's seminal **De Docta Ignorantia**, and was already clear in the work of Pythagoreans such as Archytas, and of Plato, the actual experimental demonstration of this underlying principle of all competent modern physical science, is owed to the concrete work of Kepler. Hence, Albert Einstein's celebrated argument in support of both Kepler and Riemann.

U.S. Civil War. One notable grandfather was a descendant of members of the group of the English settlers in North America during the middle of the Seventeenth Century; another was the son of a Scottish professional dragoon, a dragoon who arrived to volunteer his Civil War service with the First Rhode Island cavalry. The specifically English strain in that ancestry, was represented by grandparents representing families which had included active leaders of the anti-slavery conspiracy of their time,[5] as known to my grandparents' family dinner-table of my childhood, as having been expressed from among living ancestors born during the immediate, Seventeenth-Century establishment of what was to become this Federal republic, who were of this subsuming category.[6] In general, excepting large chunks of Scottish and Irish strains introduced to the ranks from approximately the middle of the Nineteenth Century, my family history is traced from its beginnings within North America, from Seventeenth-Century French and English immigrants from the same era as the original New England and Quebec settlements.

At the same time, the fact was, as actually known to me, that: despite a significant diversity of the specific traits and views of these individual parts of that extended family as a social process, the larger social process which was my emerging new nation (in actuality) during those three centuries before my own time, had predominant, manifestly underlying characteristics which are distinct from those of citizens of European nations, characteristics which influenced the individual representatives who were often not notably conscious of the nature of these influences upon their behavior, but which, nonetheless, were influenced by them in critical ways. Those characteristics were rooted in, as subsumed by the dynamics of this society, rather than the opinions specific to any individual representative of the family or related larger grouping. While the individual had an affect on the evolution of the national culture, the culture was never the simple aggregate of individual opinions among the population: *dynamics, again.*[7]

The most significant of the differences between the cultures of our United States and representatives of the same language-groups in Europe, was our separation from the European and other class-distinctions common to European, and such other expressions of oligarchical models of society, including those of British and other parliamentary systems.[8]

On this account, I now turn your attention to refer, once again, as I have often done so over the course of the most recently preceding sixty-odd years portion of my eighty-six years to date, to the strong impact of my first experience of the concluding paragraph of Percy Shelley's *A Defence of Poetry*, a paragraph featuring his summary on the subject of the imagination.[9] I emphasize the usually unwitting role of most relevant persons in their fostering what can be isolated as those superb moments of achievement of a great people summoned to a great task, moments in which those individual persons performed with a certain commitment and excellence, yet, often, were unwitting of the underlying source of their inspiration, when, often, as Shelley emphasized, that inspiration was even contrary to their customary character. The emergence of the U.S. population under the leadership of President Franklin D. Roosevelt, is an excellent illustration of this. Consider the ironies of the matter in Shelley's own terms.[10]

---

lutions and other developments by a society which take most of that society by surprise, when those strata see the unintended effects which their expressed opinion had created.

8. The oligarchical currents within our U.S.A. have been limited, chiefly, to the families associated with the British East India Company, and, a variant of that, the slaveholder pseudo-culture of the U.S. Federal states in which chattel slavery came to be promoted.

9. "Imagination," as employed here, does not signify "unreal;" it signifies products of the functions of the mind, rather than of mere sense-perception as such. As in all valid expressions of Classical poetry and drama, the imagination is the substance of the idea, called *irony*, whereas the relevant sense-perception is the shadow. One does not recognize one's beloved by sense-perception as such, but through those powers of the imagination needed to distinguish the person from the mere sensory form of image, as for the case of a "changeling." Irony, including metaphor, typifies this. Objects which exist, but are sensed directly only as microscopic, or sub-microscopic, are typical of this. Shelley's *A Defence of Poetry* is clear on the matter of this distinction.

10. This present report is a continuation, but in broader terms, of my own. Lyndon H. LaRouche, Jr., "The Lesson of Pearl Harbor Day," *EIR*, Dec. 19, 2008. I emphasize the presently urgent, following excerpt, taken from that paragraph which I have often quoted, orally and in print, more or less in full from Shelley (the *Harvard Classics* edition in my possession and use during the middle of the 1930s and early 1940s). I quote myself, thus, as quoting Shelley repeatedly over decades, as follows: "…we live among such philosophers and poets as surpass beyond comparison any who have appeared since the last na-

---

5. Such as the Daniel Wood who had run an "underground railway station" in Delaware County, Ohio.

6. An American family of English ancestry identified, chiefly, within a genealogical study known as "The Lancaster Family."

7. Herein lies the root of the common failures of the customary opinion-pollsters. They mistake the footprint left by the mind, for the living foot which had left that print, a print which was often a misleading indication of the intention which that print reflected. Hence, we have revo-

The fact of the often unwitting quality of the motive to which Shelley refers, within that concluding paragraph, as in the behavior of many others of his time, expresses the same phenomenon which is the subject of this, my present report. That same quality of customary individual unwittingness to which Shelley referred there, is also expressed in physical science, as, also, in what are nonetheless great artistic endeavors generally.

## The Classical Poetry of Science

Consider a more general expression of that irony.

That form of science which had been emerging from the rising waters of the oceans, then at a time not less than about 11,000 years ago,[11] was the product of what had been the ancient transoceanic maritime culture which had become settled, since, on the newly defined coastlines and the lowest regions found in the mouths of great riparian systems.

*Percy Bysshe Shelley; engraving based on Amelia Curran's painting.*

What we have come to call "science," as it emerged thus, was expressed, at that time, as that to which India's Bal Gangadhar Tilak would point, in his *Orion*, as the approximately 26,000-year Equinoctial calendar cycle already known to the ancient Vedic culture. This is a culture whose work is embedded in the cultural characteristics, even those characteristics of the presently unwitting, of both later Sanskrit and India's culture generally, amid its living population, still today. Typical human experience with such relatively long cycles, reflects ancient ocean-going maritime cultures, whose attention to the cyclical and quasi-cyclical stellar array, bespeaks a current of experience and knowledge in mankind's culture, whose emphasis on the ancient fruits of *astronavigation*[12] implicitly defines *the notion of man in, and acting efficiently upon the universe:* a true, anti-Euclidean notion of a quality of a science, which is to be defined, thus, as characteristically universal.

It is the relative mastery of this maritime standpoint for the definition of the concept of "universe," which presents the basis, from the past, for what we may fairly consider to be, virtually, the still living ancient "ancestor" of competent scientific practice, as reflected in the form of efficient action upon the domain of the here and now.

---

tional struggle for civil and religious liberty. The most unfailing herald, companion, and follower of the awakening of a great people to work a beneficial change in opinion or institution, is poetry. At such periods, there is an accumulation of the power of communicating and receiving profound and impassioned conceptions respecting man and nature. The persons in whom this power resides, may often, as far as regards many portions of their nature, have little apparent correspondence with that spirit of good of which they are the ministers. But even whilst they deny and abjure, they are yet compelled to serve, the power which is seated upon the throne of their own soul. It is impossible to read the compositions of the most celebrated writers of the present day without being startled with the electric life which burns within their words. They measure the circumference and sound the depths of human nature with a comprehensive and all-penetrating spirit, and they are themselves perhaps the most sincerely astonished at its manifestations: for it is less their spirit than the spirit of the age . . . ." That passage must be restated, in print and sung aloud, repeatedly, for the sake of its unique relevance as being uttered by me, yet once again, as stating a principle which is typical of every culture, in every age: that the individual member of society should become able to recognize himself, or herself, as expressing a behavior which is often, predominantly, typical of the movement of his, or her time, rather than simply a conscious product of his own, individual opinion-making. (My punctuation and editing.) Without that concluding paragraph of his *A Defence of Poetry*, any reprint of Shelley's piece were fraudulent by intent.

11. N.B., during the ebb in that glacial continuum estimated by some as about the recent two millions years, which is on the rise, again, today.

---

12. The original reference to experience from which the meaning of the term *astronavigation* should be derived is not essentially "space-travel," but forms of transoceanic navigation which take into account the effects specific to changes in specific astronomical experiences, from fixed to variable, which are relevant to transoceanic navigation within what had appeared, initially, as a permanently fixed set of changes within the ordering of the planets or specifically stellar phenomena. The Classical name for a practiced body of physical science so defined, is that Egyptian-Greek science of *Sphaerics*, associated with the Pythagoreans and the method of Plato. For example, any truly universal physical principle is, contrary to all empiricist doctrine, the image of a reflection of any change in the universe, local or other, whose efficient origin, as a principle of action, lies within the existence of the universe as a whole. The Vedic record of the Equinoctial cycle, as reported from seemingly landlocked central Asia, reveals its ancient maritime origins and relations to cycles within our planet's presently continuing ice-age.

*However, as I shall emphasize in the course of this present report, the proper primary subject of science, is not that of astronomy as such; science is the expression of that whose very existence is shown, essentially, not in the stars which Shakespeare brushed aside in his **Julius Caesar**,* but in a certain uniqueness of mankind's own behavior: a uniqueness which is to be adduced from in our species' unique, historical concern with ancient maritime culture's mastery of universalized astronavigation as such.[13] We must proceed from mastery of the discovered principles which the outlook of ancient mariners' astronavigation reveal, as what we must know and employ as the principles which order the development of our universe in both the respectively very large and very small. Man is not an object in the universe; man comes not merely to know the principles which order the universe, but principles which are expressed by us, as in our making that universe itself our subject (rather than ourselves as being merely the subject of that universe). *In other words: man and woman of **Genesis** 1 as in the image of the Creator.*

Thus, I shall emphasize, that, therefore, the subject of man lies, as Shakespeare wrote in his **Julius Caesar**: not in those "stars, but in ourselves," as every true Promethean must discover his, or her true heritage as a human being. Hence, true tragedy, including the intentional use of the concept of tragedy by Aeschylus, Shakespeare, and Friedrich Schiller, is not a matter of what not only ignorant, but also mis-educated individuals, label "the tragic individual." *Tragedy* is that principled quality of systemic folly which tends to permeate the "axiomatic-like" behavioral presumptions of an entire social formation, such as a language culture, a nation, or a social class, or the like, as an experience within or among nations.[14] As Shelley wrote: "…they

are themselves perhaps the most sincerely astonished at its manifestations: for it is less their spirit, than the spirit of the age. … " Mankind distinguishes itself from the beasts by superseding the spirit of a former age.

Thus, I emphasize: Johannes Kepler's uniquely original discovery of the principle of universal solar gravitation, as Albert Einstein emphasized Kepler's uniquely original discovery, as being the foundation of all competent modern experimental physical science known by Einstein and relevant others up to that time. That is the most crucial of the discoveries on which all competent modern science currently depends.

In the end, man does not react to the universe; man reacts in ways implicitly intended, as a matter of principle, to modify that universe's behavior, ultimately to qualitative effect. So, man as a species is distinguished from the beasts, if and when he chooses to do so. That is that end which a person's search for a choice of destiny must serve.

## The Evil in Euclid

The most significant of the typical causes for the intellectual failure of a promising social movement, such as the Classical Renaissance associated with that period of the American Revolution prior to the effects of the British Foreign Office's orchestration of Philippe Egalité in the incident of the Bastille, is that the fact that so many among those supporters of the cause of our American Revolution were reacting to that development, during the best preceding period, in a manner contrary to what might be fairly described as their customary inclinations. In great moments of history, a people rises above its habitual traits; but, in decadent moments, reverts to something like that which it had already been before. I saw this reversion on my return to the post-Franklin Roosevelt U.S.A., after the war. Heinrich Heine's clear insight, as in the matter of the Romantic School, into a certain moral duplicity in the impressively brilliant Goethe, illustrates the point.[15]

---

13. Long-term changes in the composition of the observed astrophysical system itself.

14. In a competent view, or performance of any Classical tragedy, the tragic factor lies in the adopted cultural habits shared among virtually an entire class of people, or the culture as a whole at that time; the individual's character is tragic only to the degree that he, or she is controlled by a habituated notion of principled behavior shared by an entire class of people, or as a "species-like" principle permeating even the culture of the population as a whole. In physical science, for example, belief in the *a-priori* elements of **Euclid's Elements**, embodies what must be recognized as a society's tragedy, that in the same general sense that the opening two paragraphs and concluding sentence of Bernhard Riemann's 1854 habilitation dissertation (the virtual "book-ends" of that composition as a whole) discredit the tragedy characteristic of Euclid's admirers. Such principled distinctions, point out almost any kind of a popular folly of an entire population, that in fashion often suggesting the

common, controlling feature subsuming the process of a slime-mold.

15. The actual downturn in the rate of immediate progress of the American Revolution, came with Lord Shelburne's role in the 1782 establishment of the British Foreign Office. Thus, Shelburne caused the negotiation of a peace treaty to divide the U.S.A., French, and Spanish allies by separate British negotiations with each. The special relationships, between Shelburne and his lackeys Jeremy Bentham and Edward Gibbon on the British side, and the set of such as Philippe Egalité, Philippe's Swiss banking crony Jacques Necker, and the Martinist freemasonry generally, on the other, triggered the setting and unfolding of the history of the world, from the siege of the Bastille, on, under what has been

Consider the historically ironical patterns of development, as during that interval of the rising influence of Abraham Kästner, his protégé Gotthold Lessing, and Moses Mendelssohn, which typify the favorable European setting for the success of the American Revolution.

The principle of that Classical school had held a large degree of sway, against the follies of the contrary influence, over strata which were, otherwise, of the contrary inclination of the Cartesian Abbé Antonio Conti, and such among Conti's followers as the hoaxsters and haters of Leibniz as Voltaire, and as the followers of Paolo Sarpi's tradition among the mere mathematicians Abraham de Moivre, Jean le Rond D'Alembert, Leonhard Euler, Joseph Lagrange, Pierre-Simon Laplace, Cauchy, Rudolf Clausius et al. That classical influence waned with the collapse of the dynamic expression of authority associated with the cause of the American Revolution, a corrosion already under way in 1782, and aggravated by the death of Benjamin Franklin, and by the fall of the Bastille orchestrated by London, and by the insurgency of that reactionary party which the Habsburg Emperor was now supporting (since the affair of the Queen's necklace).

So, the influence of the Eighteenth-Century renaissance was weakened to a degree that we in the U.S.A. saw manifest in Thomas Jefferson's period of defection, as also in the bedroom of President Madison, as under the influence of the traitor and British agent Aaron Burr. Under the earlier active influence of Benjamin Franklin, Thomas Jefferson, Madison, et al., startle us, still today, with a quality which Shelley identified as "the electric life which burns within their words," but, in the late 1790s and into the second decade of the Nineteenth Century, we must recognize the greatness of their time of association with Franklin as expressing, like the Biblical Jonah, or the Apostle Peter's "thrice," "less their spirit, than the spirit of that age." So, in the matter of the so-called "Monroe Doctrine," and other matters of later life, Jefferson returned to himself as he had been, more or less, under the influence of his former mentor, Benjamin Franklin.

Any truly competent treatment of history must recognize the kinds of examples which I have just referenced here, and also recognize the principle which Shelley had addressed in what I have referenced here as the relationship between the individual and the motivating power which appears in the form of the "spirit of the age."

So, we experienced a comparable return to the worse, with the death of President Franklin Roosevelt. Already, once the Normandy victory of the U.S.-led allies assured the defeat of the Nazis, the same, British led, right-wing faction, inside the U.S.A., which had been pro-Mussolini-Hitler prior to December 7, 1941, moved to take back their former power. So, the death of President Franklin Roosevelt served as the opportunity for the former, pro-fascist, right-wing gang to regain power in the Presidency under President Truman. During most of that change back toward a "right-wing" takeover of U.S. leadership, I was overseas—until late Spring 1946, and therefore had the peculiar "advantage" of experiencing, more fully, the shock of that change within U.S. institutions which had taken over the U.S.A. during the interval from Spring 1945 to Spring 1946.

The weakness of otherwise promising figures of the U.S.A., which allowed the corruption expressed by the "Wall Street" phenomenon, is also to be recognized in the pro-fascist elements of "right wing" anti-Franklin Roosevelt circles, particularly those which had been openly pro-Mussolini during both the 1920s and 1930s and sympathizers of Hitler during the pre-December 1941 1930s, and which represent the Liberal "free trader" tradition of the pro-fascist elements of both the Republican and Democratic parties still today.

We are currently experiencing a turn, somewhat akin to that under the onset of Franklin Roosevelt's leadership, in the early days of the change of the U.S. Presidency, from the reign of the wretched President George W. Bush, Jr., to the spirit of optimism which has arisen since the inauguration of the Presidency of newly incumbent President Barack Obama. We must reckon with both of the implications which that change presents, and do so with accompanying comprehension of what I have just summarized here as the thesis of Percy B. Shelley. The present moment is precious, its opportunities prospectively grand, and the perils grave.

This, as I have promised above, will be, necessarily, a lesson on the higher implications of the principles of dynamics.

---

called "The British Empire," from 1782 to the present day. The British East India Company's empire was established in fact, as a private empire of that company, by the February 1763 Peace of Paris; but, the systemic features of the government of that empire were established by Shelburne's adoption of Gibbon's model of Julian the Apostate.

The end of the Second World War is celebrated in Norfolk, Virginia, 1945. Already, a shift was underway in the "spirit of the age."

National Archives

National Archives and Records Administration

*Veterans returning from the war settled with their families into suburban bungaloes, retreating from the great cause for which they had recently fought.*

Library of Congress

*With the death of FDR, the right-wing crowd regained power in the Presidency and other institutions. Here, the fascist Sen. Joseph McCarthy and his lawyer, Roy Cohn, during the Army-McCarthy hearings in 1954.*

## I. Dynamics & Immortality

*Yes, young fellow, human immortality does exist, just not biologically. You could say, that, in that way, it has an efficient, practical expression within the individual's and society's experience of mortal life. Thus, true immortality is not something to be relegated to some domain of blind faith; it not only can, but must be experienced by every living person who knows, really, what it is to be immortal, and, to be, thus, human in the sense of man and woman of **Genesis** 1. It exists for us within a very efficient domain of experience, one called by Leibniz, and by others, dynamics. It is important that you discover this fact for yourself, so that you may discover not only how to act as human, but how to become truly, fully human, not as some talking simulation of a higher ape, but as the realization of becoming a fully human, implicitly immortal being.*

There are several crucial points to be considered in this summary of the case.

1. First, and foremost, the essential distinction of the human personality from all among the beasts: that human personality is expressed by a living body with ostensible animal characteristics; but that, as the effect of the outstanding creative personalities of science and Classical art illustrate this more clearly, the creative human personality will continue to influence the development of the quality of society in a specifically creative way, as a sovereign personality, even after the mortal body of that person is dead.

So, the incompleted discovery of one person can be adopted and extended in an active way after that person is deceased. So, each creative individual lives as represented in the continuing development of society even after the death of the mortal husk.

2. Thus, that human society is not a collection of individuals, but is dynamic, not merely

percussive, in respect to the interaction of society's individual members.

3. That the progress of society depends upon forms of action by individuals which express a form of action of change of culture comparable to the effect of the discovery and adoption of a universal physical principle, that according to such models as Johannes Kepler's uniquely original discovery of the principle of universal gravitation.

So, for example, the principal failures which those who were merely mathematicians have brought into the domain of physical science, are results which could be traced readily, by some, from what has been clearly the outright fraud prompted, still, to the present day, by the *a-priori* presumptions of **Euclid's Elements**. These failures have been rooted in the *a-priori* notion, that both space (explicitly) and time (implicitly) are as Euclid's almost bestial *a-priori* assumptions of sense-perception wrongly presume them to be.

However, since the work of such leading modern scientists as Riemann, Planck, and Einstein, the absurd notions of *space* which may be associated with the legacy of Euclid, have been called more seriously into question. Nonetheless, even among the so-called scientifically literate classes, a mistaken notion of *time*, considered as being consistent with the presumption of simple clock-time, maintains its stubborn grip on belief, even among some considered to be leading physical scientists.

The matter of time is the crucial theme of this present report on the principles of economy.

Nonetheless, despite those reasons for doubts, even among scientists, respecting the notion of simple clock-time, even on the most rudimentary level of the notion of dynamics, the popular tendency has been, as it might be said: to "go along with the popular notion of clock-time,

Library of Congress

*Gottfried Wilhelm Leibniz (1646-1716) anticipated Einstein's study of space-time: "The source of our difficulties with the composition of the continuum comes from the fact that we think of matter and space as substance, whereas in themselves material things are merely well-regulated phenomena, and space is exactly the same as the order of coexistence, as time is the order of existence which is not simultaneous." (Letter to Nicholas Resmond, March 14, 1714.)*

to all practical intents and purposes." It is not until we pause to examine more closely the way in which human creativity functions in the effects of fundamental progress in physical science, or, also, the Classical metaphor of poetry and musical counterpoint, the more we begin to recognize the existence of a practicable approach to comprehension of this ironical character of the human experience of time as such: the *physical time of evolutionary change in the rate of human action per capita and per square kilometer at the Earth's surface, rather than clock time.*

To introduce this point most simply, and yet forcefully, consider the following.

The long reign of a Euclidean or similar pseudo-science, as within what is usually studied as ancient through modern European history, is echoed in the role of those arbitrary, *a-priori,* assumptions respecting space and time, which are, as I have just stated, above, associated with the same state of mind as faith in the fraudulent dogma of **Euclid's Elements**, that as according to what are still those popularly accepted, but incompetent presumptions.

On the first account of those popular, but mistaken beliefs, the notion of *space,* the notion of an infinite Euclidean, or Cartesian space, is not acceptable in anything which should be allowed to pass for modern scientific method among respectable sorts of relevant modern institutions. Space put to one side; so, far, however, most opinion on the meaning of time is still worse than muddy, even among professionals. This failure by them has crucial bearing on the reasons for the failures of economists and relevant others so far today.

So, despite the clear case respecting the falseness of belief in "space by itself, or time by itself," as made by such authorities as Albert Einstein, the needed correction for the notion of *physical time* (rather than "clock time") has not become anything better than can be met among a tiny fraction of what passes for literate expressions of contemporary scientific opinion.

In outlining that case here, my emphasis is on the importance of a relativistic conception of physical time, as needed for competent argument in the field of a science of physical economy. This, however, is not merely the kind of a formal problem to be relegated to the classroom. My emphasis here is on the role of relativistic time in the practical work of that science of physical-economy which is my speciality. In that latter context, it points toward the implied requirements of the highly practical need for my own choice of a broader, and more profound approach to the notion of time urgently needed in the common practice of nations today.

Currently, the most damaging error in the usual treatment of the subject of time, among even some persons formally certified as scientists, occurs chiefly as the expression of a widespread hoax, a dubious notion of thermodynamics which is traced to the supposed "authority" of the mid-Nineteenth-Century activities of mechanistic dogmatists such as Rudolf Clausius, Hermann Grassmann, Lord Kelvin, and the later followers of Ernst Mach and, worse, Bertrand Russell. The "pro-Malthusian" form of political motive for that fraud, known as "The Second Law of Thermodynamics," is as interesting clinically, and important, as it is related to the study of the closely related implications of the popular folly, even among scientists, on the subject of time.

I will return to that popular error in due course, here. First, I must define the issue as it is posed from the standpoint of the working scientist; in this case, I mean the standpoint of economic science, my profession, rather than mistaken appeals to the favor of today's wildly misguided popular opinion on that subject .

Therefore, we must now work through the following discussion of some key features of the problem.

In the rudimentary physics of design in construction, for example, we consider the specific relationship of the geometry of supporting structures, to the required mass of support required for the combined mass of both that support and that which it supports. The Paris Eiffel Tower is among the most conspicuous illustrations of this point, still for today. My own introduction to that physical view of geometry, came to me about the time I reached the age of fourteen, a consequence of my fascination with this ironical feature of the structures witnessed at the neighboring Boston area's Charlestown

*The magnificent construction of the Eiffel Tower illustrates LaRouche's point that geometry is not a question of blackboard mathematics, but of structure in the physical universe.*

Navy Yard. As a result of that experience, I had rejected the notion of Euclidean geometry at my first secondary classroom encounter with it, and, as a result of that, soon became an admirer of some translated works of Gottfried Leibniz, that in some not-unimportant, relevant respects.

In the science of physical economy, the same type of point is illustrated in the matter of the functional relationship of the infrastructure which supports production and its productivity, to the specific effect, that, obviously, infrastructure which supports no *physically productive* function by mankind, is waste, or, might be described as comparable to the role of the fruits of the act of masturbation in the production of society's wealth.[16]

---

16. The apologist might argue that, it may not be productive, but it might be considered as threatening to produce, even without ever producing what its advocate purports to simulate. The Rockefeller Foundation's recent proposal to perpetrate the public display of "economic masturbation for a price" in supporting the "infrastructure" swindle of New York's Mayor Bloomberg and Californication's Governor Arnold Schwarzenegger, is an illustration of the principle involved.

So much, so far, on background, for the matter of the physical function of space. What of the physical-economic function of time?

## Creativity as Human

Insofar as our attention is focused upon the notion of the "creation of wealth," this signifies something which, in the view of competent animal ecologists, never occurs within the bounds of practice of any animal species, except through effects of biological evolution. Willful creativity never occurs except through the creative intervention of the human will, as by farmers, for example. Consider the contrasting cases of the so-called "animal kingdom" and society on account of this difference between man and beast.

Fairly said, in the study of animal populations, but not in the case of mankind, the potential relative population-density of animal species, is not located essentially in the willful powers of the particular species, but, rather, in an ecology within the evolution of the Biosphere as a whole, integrated (dynamic) process. Thus, for example, the application of the specific idea of an animal ecology to mankind, is an intention and practice of a type, which, in the case of human society, would be tantamount to forms of fascism such as that Hitler-like, "green fascism" of Prince Philip's pro-genocidal World Wildlife Fund: a practice whose utopian expression is best described as "farming human populations" as one does flocks of hens or herds of cattle. Adolf Hitler and Hermann Göring, like the lately deceased former Nazi-SS officer Prince Bernhard of the Netherlands, and his fellow Prince Philip accomplice, former U.S. Vice-President Al Gore, typify their intended application, as by the World Wildlife Fund, of the ecological principles of mere animal populations to people.

That view by such as that Prince Philip, the late Prince Bernhard, and Al Gore, is otherwise expressed

Courtesy of Pennie Sabel

*Filippo Brunelleschi introduced the physical principle of the catenary, to craft the great cupola of the Cathedral of Florence. Lower left, a cutaway shows the interior structure.*

in the perverted, already implicitly fascist notion of the contemporary descendants of Giammaria Ortes, and of his plagiarist Thomas Malthus, that the notion of "balance" within systems of animal ecologies must be also imposed upon human populations.

We should not be surprised that this shameless, shared dogma of so-called "eugenics," as shared among the late Bertrand Russell and Aldous Huxley, Prince Philip, the late Prince Bernhard, and former Vice-President Al Gore, is approximately as incompetent for science, as it is as monstrous as it was in the paws of Hitler and Göring,, when applied to humanity.

From the relevant standpoint of physical science, the essential functional difference between human and animal populations, is located in those potentially creative powers of human individual reason which are absent from all members of animal ecologies. Hence, we have Academician V.I. Vernadsky's distinction of Noösphere from Biosphere, to the following effect.[17]

## As Seen in Physical Science Generally

At this point in our account, we must introduce an illustration of the functional meaning of creativity; the most appropriate approximation for that immediate purpose, is that uniqueness of Johannes Kepler's discovery of the principle of universal gravitation, as in his *The Harmonies of the World*. This work of Kepler serves at this point in my account, to point out the shocking incompetence of today's customary academic use of the term "creativity," as the contrary, true character of this discovery by Kepler was treated properly by Albert Einstein, as being the foundation of competence in modern, Riemannian, European physical science.

On that account, I must, therefore, insert a qualification for what is to be said now. This qualification is, that all competent modern science is Riemannian in that coincidental sense of the use of the term "Riemannian" by both Einstein's treatment of the subject of Kepler's astronomy, and in the related case of Academician V.I. Vernadsky's defining of the physical chemistry of the Noösphere. The coincidence of intention expressed in these and related cases, hangs on that notion of dynamics which had been brought back to life, so to speak, by Gottfried Leibniz's defining the meaning of "dynamics" in connection with his attack on the incompetence of Descartes and, implicitly, also, Descartes' Seventeenth-Century and later empiricist

*Academician Vladimir I. Vernadsky (1863-1945), the Ukrainian-Russian biogeochemist who pioneered the Soviet Union's nuclear program. His work, including his concept of the "Noösphere," is rooted in Riemannian physics.*

followers.[18] The list of such relevant rogues as those empiricists, includes the philosophical mechanists Clausius and Grassman, Ernst Mach, and, most emphatically, the hoaxster Bertrand Russell.

By the term "creativity," I mean such relevant historical occurrences as the duplication of the cube by Plato's contemporary Archytas; and, such modern cases as the discovery, by Filippo Brunelleschi, of the function of the physical principle of the catenary, as to be seen, still today, in the principle of design employed for the construction of the cupola of Florence's Santa Maria del Fiore; as to be read in the founding of the system of modern European physical science by Cardinal Nicholas of Cusa in his *De Docta Ignorantia*, or, in the uniquely original discovery of universal gravitation by Johannes Kepler; or, the principle of least action by Pierre de Fermat; and, the uniquely original discovery of the modern calculus by Gottfried Leibniz. Ironically, each of these discoveries expresses a common, shared principle of creativity which subsumes each and all as aspects of a common dynamic conception, as might be anticipated for the case of a set of events expressing one and the same physical universe.

The avoidance of that error in defining creativity which each of us must be certain to ward off, requires that we stick strictly to Albert Einstein's approach to the subject of Kepler's discovery of the general principle of gravitation, as Kepler effected the original discovery, as shown in Kepler's *The Harmonies of the World*, and, then, Einstein's viewing Kepler's actual approach to that result from the standpoint of Einstein's adoption of the viewpoint of Bernhard Riemann.

---

17. Although Vernadsky was prompted to adopt the term "Noösphere" from his encounter with the use of that term by Teilhard de Chardin, the systemic features of the use of the term by Vernadsky are rooted in his application of the standpoint of Riemannian physics, not those quaintly mystical, reductionist schemes of Teilhard de Chardin, as those associated with the infamous Piltdown hoax.

18. Such as "the usual suspects" Abbé Antonio Conti, Abraham de Moivre, Jean le Rond D'Alembert, Leonhard Euler, Joseph Lagrange, Pierre-Simon Laplace, and the sometime plagiarist and hoaxster Augustin Cauchy.

NOAA/Shane Anderson

**The abiotic:** *Dramatic rock formations on Santa Cruz Island, one of California's Channel Islands—but with the biosphere clearly making its incursions.*

NOAA/Channel Islands NMS

**The biosphere:** *Garibaldi damselfish (*Hypsypops rubicundus*) live around the Channel Islands.*



NOAA/Joe Heath

**The Noösphere:** *young scientists, exploring the tidepools at Moss Beach, Calif.*

The risk of error lies in acceptance of the misleading assumption, that a principle of nature is defined by numerical values for an algebraic function, when, in fact, as for the case of Kepler's uniquely original discovery of gravitation, exactly the opposite relationship between principle and coefficient pertained. Any actually universal physical principle does not lie within the system; but, as Einstein insisted, it bounds it, that in the same sense that Einstein emphasizes, that in opposition to the pseudo-science of modern, Sarpian philosophical Liberalism, that gravitation is not a mechanical-like relationship within the system; rather, it bounds the entire system, both externally and internally, as a finite system of a form which is without external boundary at any given moment in the system's normal, continuing (*anti-entropic*) self-development.

However, to grasp certain implications which are also already embedded, if only as systemic implications, in Einstein's presentation of the case, seek the greater degree of clarity required, by taking into account V.I. Vernadsky's distinction of Noösphere from Biosphere.

Any system which does not lie within the Biosphere, lies either within the system of inherently non-living processes, or within the Noösphere which supersedes the Biosphere. No living process, or what is uniquely a relic of a living process, is a relic, as a living process, of the "pre-biotic" phase-space of our universe. Yet, no noëtic function of human mind is a specific product of the Biosphere. Yet, the universe, which contains the three, categorically distinct, and interacting phase-spaces (the *abiotic*, the *Biosphere*, and the *Noösphere*), which thus expresses a universal (creative) principle of anti-entropy, subsumes the three phase-spaces. That universe is intrinsically anti-entropic in and of itself, and imparts that inherently noëtic quality to that integrated process which it contains. Such a set of conclusions, is supported by the evidence of the accomplishments most distinctly characteristic of the creative powers (acting within the dynamic of society as such), the anti-entropy which is the characteristic seed-form of the human mind itself.

Nothing demonstrates those principles more clearly, more emphatically, than the subject of a science of physical economy. Such is the implication of the notion of mankind's individual as a noëtic power of change within the universe.

*Noësis*—that quality which true human creativity shares with the universe as a whole—is a principle in itself. By *noësis*, we signify an action of the type which adds a new principled element to the universe, such as the knowledge of the discovery of what is, for that person, a previously unknown, *lawful quality of* principle of the universe, as typified by Kepler's uniquely original discovery of universal gravitation, as presented by him in his **The Harmonies of the World**.

All of the categorical discoveries of universal principle to which I have referred thus far, are contrary to that vile hoaxster Bertrand Russell, and are included among the dynamics of a common type of creativity. Therefore, wherever I employ the term "creativity" hereinafter, I signify that meaning of the term "creativity."

## Ecology, Economy & Creativity

The universe, insofar as we presently know it, is essentially *anti-entropic*.

Our Sun is a product of its immediate "neighborhood," that being our galaxy, which was in turn, a product of the universe as a whole. The Solar System, and its periodic table of elements and the like, are a product (of probably polarized thermonuclear fusion) generated by the evolution of a once faster-spinning, younger Sun. The preconditions for the appearance of living processes on Earth, are traced in apparently manifest origins to the development of our planet Earth. The species of life were ostensibly generated on Earth, but, probably, must have also appeared in locations such as other parts of our Solar system and beyond. The living species which wander, slither, crawl, fly, walk, or swim with apparent willfulness, on the land, within the upper crust of the Earth, and in the bodies of water, constitute an included part of what Academician V.I. Vernadsky defined for physical chemistry as a Biosphere. Into this setting came mankind. Mankind's characteristic, potential, *willful creativity*, is not found in any other known living species.

The existence of mankind thus changes the ordering principle within the universe, away from what must be assumed to be the characteristic of a universe without the existence of mankind.

The orders of life which appear amid such develop-

ments, are represented, as I have already said here, by two distinct general categories, the Biosphere and the Noösphere, as both have been defined with a certain scientific rigor by Academician Vernadsky. Although, we know of development within the Biosphere, from such orders as marsupials, to the superior placentals, no animal or comparable species of life, apart from mankind, has presented us with what can be classed as creative powers comparable to the quality which distinguishes the human species as absolutely superior, categorically, to other forms of life, even to forms generated, as ostensibly from marsupial to mammal within the domain of animal life.

*Raphael's "The School of Athens." Detail showing Plato (pointing up) and Aristotle.*

The relevant sort of gross demonstration of these distinctions of beast from man, is found in the comparison of the fixed difference of the dynamic of the biosphere as defined only by the animal species, to the breaking of such types of ecological boundaries by the presence of mankind. Man changes the value of the Biosphere, usually upward, by aid of the role of human creativity in changing the composition and anti-entropic values for the Biosphere.

## The Immortality of the Soul

In my knowledge of the matter, the idea of the immortality of the human soul, came meaningfully into the province of European physical science only as an aspect of what some currents of Judaism share with the scientific implications of Christianity.[19] My own knowledge of the history of that concept of immortality, is rooted in references to the work of Plato, and that of Cardinal Nicholas of Cusa and his followers, as that concept of the principle of human *dynamics* was illustrated as the argument famously illustrated in the Vatican Library's "School of Athens" by Raphael Sanzio.[20]

---

19. E.g. the exposure of the fraud of Aristotle by Philo of Alexandria, and the work of Moses Mendelssohn.

20. Some would say, that the figure of Plato is pointing the way to God

Any valid reading of the background for that view, pertains to the associated notion of a "simultaneity of eternity." This concept is, in turn, interchangeable, ontologically, with the notion of that human creativity which we trace in European history from the *Sphaerics* of the ancient Pythagoreans, Plato, and those of kindred insight and accomplishment. The celebrated, unique solution for the construction of the doubling of the cube, by Archytas, has been, historically, a scientifically crucial demonstration of the method of reconstructing knowledge congruent with that conception. Kepler's discovery of the general principle of gravitation, as in his ***The Harmonies of the World***, is an expression of this, as is Fermat's concept of least action, and Gottfried Leibniz's uniquely original discovery of the principle of the infinitesimal calculus.

In general, as in those instances which I have just referenced, the existence of action in physical space, like that of the infinitesimal of action in time, must replace the superstition of belief in "absolute" space and "absolute" time as such. That needed conception must be dynamic, not percussive.

The demonstration of that principle of a science of physical economy which underlies the notion of a "simultaneity of eternity," was presented in a pedagogically expert way by Philo's argument denouncing the posturing of the Aristoteleans of his time. The relevant theological argument may be properly restated as follows.

Aristotle's relevant argument is that since the Creator is perfect, the results of his work are perfect. Therefore, according to the argument of the relevant Aristotelians, once the Universe is "made," the Creator Himself could not be permitted to change it. The implication of this is, that the philosophical reductionists, of which that Aristotelean dogma is an example, would not have permitted a God who created the universe to have existed, in the first place. The point is, that the perfection of the Creation lies in the power of the Creator to change it. In other words, in real physical science, the fundamental law of the universe is the continuing power of creation: the universe is essentially an anti-entropic one, from which the concept of universal entropy is absolutely banned.

In other words, to identify the conclusion to be reached in the simplest terms: the notion of a *permanent Creator* whose existence is contrary to the Aristotelean presumption attacked by Philo, implies (if it does not yet suffice to prove) the notion of a fixed conceptual reference-point of existence in a universe undergoing characteristically systemic transformations.

**The Role of Descartes**

For purposes of reference to modern empiricism, such as that of René Descartes and his modern dupes, let that follower of Paolo Sarpi, the thoroughly wicked Descartes, be the whipping-boy of reference for our argument here. Descartes is a follower of Paolo Sarpi, not Aristotle, but the argument against Aristotle follows for our purposes here. A brief comment on the historical significance of Descartes since Europe's early Eighteenth Century, is required, to situate historically what we have to say today.

Descartes is, with one important qualification, the model used by Abbé Antonio Conti and others for the crafting of the synthetic personality of Sir Isaac Newton. The circle of fakers associated immediately with Newton was created chiefly as a faction intended to combat, even intended to eradicate the reputations of Johannes Kepler, Pierre de Fermat, Leibniz, and, to some degree, Christiaan Huyghens. The most significant target selected by the followers of Paolo Sarpi, during the Eighteenth Century and beyond, was Gottfried Leibniz. The desire for Leibniz's ruin, during the 1690s and beyond, a desire premised on the intention to defend the principal features of the claimed authority of Descartes, was the chief motivating factor in that work of a network of salons created to promote the reputation of the synthetic personality of Sir Isaac Newton, a project which was initiated by Abbé Antonio Conti and Voltaire, and implemented through a network of salons featuring Abraham de Moivre, Jean le Rond D'Alembert, Leonhard Euler, Euler's intellectual protégé Joseph Lagrange, and such as Pierre-Simon Laplace, Augustin Cauchy, Clausius, Grassmann, and Lord Kelvin.

After considering all features of that campaign by Conti et al. which are relevant for our consideration of the subject of the present chapter here, it is the neo-Euclidean conception of ontologically empty space and ontologically empty time, as defined by the follower of the Paolo Sarpi school's René Descartes, which fills the vacancy of the thought in physical and popular science for the presently still hegemonic, and popular empiricist school of leading trans-Atlantic opinion about scientific matters, still today. Even where the impact of

---

the Creator, while Aristotle, in a like manner, is directing his minions to Hell. I believe that Philo would agree strongly with me on that point.

Nineteenth-Century progress in continental European science has threatened to supplant the axiomatic, Cartesian notion of "Cartesian empty space," there is almost no significant progress, yet, in attention to the evidence exposing the fraud of the Euclidean-like "empty space" of clock-time.

To understand the origins and characteristics of the fallacious notions of space and time being examined in this moment, the following, very ancient implications of the fraud by Descartes and his followers must be considered here.

## Clausius' Crime Against Science

The most conspicuous obstacle to recognizing the reality of *physical time*, rather than clock time, has become the fraudulent assertion introduced, as the popularized cult of that mechanistic doctrine of thermodynamics premised on the initiative of Rudolf Clausius, the mathematician Hermann Grassmann, and their associate Lord Kelvin.[21] What inspired Clausius et al. is appropriately located as an echo of the argument by the fictional Olympian Zeus of Aeschylus' **Prometheus Bound,** in which Zeus menaces all mortal persons, pagan gods, and demi-gods alike with threat of the torture meted out to Prometheus, should anyone dare to inform mortal mankind of the existence of discoverable universal physical principles, such as "fire," by means of which human potential might be increased in fact.

Although Aeschylus's report is one of the greatest Classical compositions in all of the known history of European civilization, what Aeschylus attributes to the mouth of Zeus is, in historical fact, the greatest political and moral issue in the known history of mankind, even still today. What is being expressed by Aeschylus' character Zeus, as by Clausius, Grassmann, and Kelvin, ranks among the cruelest frauds against science and mankind in the sum-total of known history to date; such is the effect of the doctrine known since Clausius, as *universal entropy,* or, before Clausius, by creatures such as the Giammaria Ortes whose English edition was so lavishly plagiarized by Thomas Malthus.

The known origins of the oligarchical model pre-

scribed by that fictitious Zeus[22] are traced from the mists of more ancient millennia, into the rise of the type of oligarchical maritime model of both the Mediterranean region and land-based West Asia. The emerging characteristic of these cultures rooted in such ancient times, has been the model of society based upon the principle of human cattle, cattle who talk, but not too much, on the subject of the authority of what are esteemed as the pagan "god-like" or "semi-god-like," who are assigned the function of more or less arbitrary rule, a rule by flesh-and-blood demi-gods, whose power is limited by the still higher power of the pleasure of mythical invisible gods. The Homeric **Iliad** and **Odessey** are contrasted cases which illustrate the role of the tradition of such pagan gods and demi-gods, still today.

So, the idea of the Roman Pantheon, and of the British empire struck in the model of Julian the Apostate, are illustrations of the reality of that pagan tradition, even if the visibly reigning authorities are not any real gods, but, merely the incarnate demi-gods of ruling social-political classes, classes which do as much as they can to promote adoration and fear of the alleged, invisible hand of the pagan gods of the City of London and Wall Street.

To create and maintain organizations of society in which the majority of the population is bestialized through a maintained status as slaves, serfs, or modern European culture's pleasure-seeking fools, it has been considered necessary by those ruling classes, or by other circles of similar bent, to stupefy the general population into suitable states of submission, preferably self-induced submission to a conditioned culture which acts as invisible shackles on the mind of those intended to submit by self-inflicted habits and related ways of thinking. The indoctrination of foolish believers in **Euclid's Elements** must be prominently included as an example of this.

---

21. See **Bernhard Riemanns Gesammelte Mathematische Werke**, H. Weber, ed. (New York: Dover Publications reprint, 1953), footnote on p. 293. The posthumous attack on Riemann's work, by editor Heinrich Weber there, is premised on the presumed authority of Clausius, although the argument was actually made by Clausius' associate, the mathematician Grassmann. The significance of this matter is located in the text of the body of this report, above.

22. It is to be conceded that there is an argued, and likely historical basis for that model of the Olympian Zeus, as the Roman (Sicilian) chronicler Diodorus Siculus attributes the information to both Egyptian chronicles and the legends of the Berbers of his own time. The Middle Eastern documentation traces the origin of the oligarchical model referenced as the case of the Zeus of Aeschylus's **Prometheus Bound** to its exemplification by the degeneration of the bow-tenure system of an Indian Ocean-based maritime culture from the Fourth Millenium B.C., which degenerated, and was replaced by an emerging Semitic culture, which became, in turn, the root of the Babylonian and related oligarchical models of later times.

**The Prometheus Concept**

This problem was understood, in his fashion, by the Cardinal Nicholas of Cusa whose earlier *Concordancia Catholica* and *De Docta Ignorantia* have been prominent keystones on which Europe's escape from the Fourteenth-Century "New Dark Age" has depended, even to the extent this has happened thus far. Among the most crucial of the included contributions of Cusa, were expressed in his *De Pace Fidei*, the peace of faiths, and his crucial part in setting forth the policy which set Christopher Columbus on the course for discovery of the Americas. That is to emphasize, on the last account, that Cusa's recognition of the pernicious role of the Venetian financier oligarchy in its effort to destroy the great, mid-Fifteenth Century European renaissance, required crossing the oceans to develop Europe's relations on other continents. Columbus, who encountered and adopted this policy of Cusa's, about 1480 A.D., thus produced the initiative which led the best currents of Europe to taking, hopefully, some of the best of Europe's culture to a distant place of relative safety, freed from the immediate grip of Europe's, essentially financier-controlled oligarchy.

The fortunate outcome of that was the founding of the U.S. Federal constitutional republic; the unfortunate thing, was that the European financier and related oligarchies pursued the European colonies across the oceans, and sought to bring about their permanent submission to European oligarchical corruption, as imperial London's creation, the North American Confederacy, was formed to this purpose, and London's pet, Wall Street, has continued this predatory role of seduction and other corruption under a just ended, monstrously morally and financially corrupt U.S. Presidency from whose induced state of wreckage we are now struggling to arise again.

Yet, all that, and much more said to the same effect, the nature of the human individual, as distinct from the nature of all lower forms of life, is shown to be efficient, in that the inherent creative powers, and inborn character of the human individual, has produced an improvement in the size and condition of the human population in general, and has also given us the means of potential to succeed in reaching levels of achievement never known by any other species during, or before our present time.

The actuality, and, more significantly, the potentiality for such continued achievement lives within and among us today. All of this achievement, and all potential for future achievement, depend upon the truth of that spoken by the fictional Prometheus of *Prometheus Bound*, and also spoken, implicitly or otherwise, by those who see in the human species a power for development which brings us toward a likeness to the Author of this universe, if we are but willing, and enabled to accept that challenge of immortality.

So, as the U.S. Declaration of Independence quoted Gottfried Leibniz's "the pursuit of happiness" in the founding of our republic, it is the goal of reconciling our purpose in existence to that outcome of our existence as personalities beyond the beastly aspect of our incarnation, which is the standpoint in personal commitment which would prompt us to yearn for a certain immortality which is expressed in sundry ways, including scientific and technological progress in the condition, and the increase of power, per capita, and per square kilometer, of the human species so destined.

**'Aye, there's the rub'**

So far, so good. However, astute readers of these lines already know, that all to be considered on this account is seldom truth or goodness. The most common experience of a person who seeks to be good in the sense I have just indicated, that from childhood, is that he, or she, when pursuing the goals of cognitive self-development toward which I have just pointed above, will often find himself, or herself the target of a "black chick, white chick" phenomenon. Will he, or she, be able to stand up for truth, when a popular or kindred lie is demanded? It is often fairly said, that the principle of torture is "sweet conformity."

"Why do students lie in school?" As Adam Smith wrote in his 1759 *Theory of the Moral Sentiments*: in pursuit of pleasure and avoidance of pain. Truth does not necessarily come up for consideration, in either classroom, or playground; what you are expected to repeat, does. Thus, in our society today, speaking truth is usually avoided, and frequently even dangerous. Being popular has its perils, but it is nonetheless the usual goal of those who are, at least temporarily, prosperous and influential, until they come upon what they come to consider the sudden injustice of their own misfortune.

It should become obvious, sooner or later, to those who have some sort of what is called "a realistic outlook," that the delusions of those who think themselves either successful, or about to become successful, are the chains of delusion through which those who think themselves on the top of things, are mustered to ride herd on those who, for the moment, are on the bottom. However, an exchange of place usually lurks nearby.

Truth lies not in the past or present, but in devotion to a better future. A "better future" usually turns out to be something which develops, as for Niccolo Machiavelli, when one is rather old, or already deceased. Wisdom is usually devotion to what a future generation should experience. This means, in turn, that happiness, in the sense of the passage from Leibniz contained with the 1776 **U.S. Declaration of Independence**, means an assurance of the future outcome of the present.

Take Shakespeare's tragedy of Hamlet as a case in point. In the famous soliloquy, "To be, or not to be," Hamlet contemplates his adopted devotion to his own doom. This is not because there is no alternative; but, there is no acceptable alternative for a member in good standing, even any official of his self-doomed society. The doom lies not within himself, but in the relevant characteristic of his society, a cage formed of the compulsions of adherence to the habit of his society, from which he is unwilling to escape completely. In Schiller's **Wallenstein** trilogy, it is not what Wallenstein does, which is his fate, but that which he does not know how to do, precisely because the evil which grips his society, is not his own, but he is a prisoner of both the culture, in the tradition of the Netherlands wars, and a prisoner of the cultural setting of the Habsburgs and Paolo Sarpi, not the Westphalian impulse of a Cardinal Mazarin. After all, Schiller's **Wallenstein** is not fiction, but the shadow of real history put on stage as historically truthful drama.

## II. Dynamics & Creativity

Since the introduction of this report as a whole, I have repeatedly emphasized, here, the decisive importance of that concept of dynamics which Leibniz had revived from the *dynamis* of Classical Greek science, as being the crucial principle upon which all competent notions of economy are to be premised. So, echoing Percy Shelley's *A Defence of Poetry*, I emphasized that the dynamic which subsumes the equivalent of the Classical musical composition as a whole, particularly that in the tradition of Johann Sebastian Bach, is the key to the whole action of which the various, subsumed elements are only subordinated aspects.

As I have pointed out repeatedly, above, the function of human creativity, as distinct from anything encountered among lower forms of life, is that once a valid discovery of principle is made, the discoverer, or his or her mentors, should be reminded to relive that act of discovery. This process of reliving the act of discovery, has a feature of crucial significance. That is, once a discovery has been made and validated in its own terms, we must return to the origin of that specific discovery, this time to rediscover the universe which has been changed by the initially successful discovery.

The point to be emphasized so, is that the nature of any valid principle of the universe is its universality. Thus, while a discovery of a principled form of action is made, we must then discover whether this takes into account all of the changes which our discovery has made *in defining the universe within which it has occurred.*

That leads to outbursts of the following relevance: "We have just made a valid discovery of what is, in its own terms, a universal principle. Since such a success, however otherwise limited, has changed our idea of the universe from what it had been a moment earlier, we must now hypothesize and experiment afresh, this time to discover the universe which has been changed from that which we had thought we knew before the new discovery was to be added to our roster."

Take cases such as Archytas' duplication of the cube, Brunelleschi's discovery of the physical principle of the catenary, Nicholas of Cusa's **De Docta Ignorantia**, Kepler's discovery of the principal of universal gravitation, Fermat's discovery of the principle of least action, and Leibniz's uniquely original discovery of the calculus, as examples. Then take all discoveries which have a similar quality of uniqueness as principles, whether in science or Classical art-forms. These typify, individually, or as combined, the kind of notions which are key to identifying the principles which subsume, and situate the composition as a unified whole effect. Each of these discoveries required the subsequent discovery of an added, principled consideration.

There is no linear (e.g., statistical) continuity in the unfolding of history.

With the introduction of this concept of dynamics, as Hermann Minkowski proposed for a reform of physics, "space by itself, and time by itself" cease to exist. (Unfortunately, the brilliant Minkowski erred in choosing Lobatchevskian geometry, rather than Riemannian.) The part then partakes of the nature of the whole, and, more than that, conveys the nature of the whole in each impact of the part.

Now, interpose the intention to act according to such a principle of dynamics in an interval of action. Such a development presents us with a form of relevant, creative action within an interval of time for that action. This defines the general meaning of relativistic time. Thus, through the role of principles of actions which transform space-time, neither space nor time are empty forms. We have, simply said, physical space-time, instead.

That application of such a conception of dynamics to social processes considered in those terms, is the true key to the principles of a practiced science of physical economy. The natural outcome of that, is that the underlying principle of a competent science of economy, and of related features of social interaction and development otherwise, is Riemannian dynamics as the work of Einstein and Vernadsky typify the role of Riemannian dynamics in all competent modern physical science.

Take a relatively simple type of action, corresponding to an included enhancement of a principle, from the process of physical production. This enhances the productive powers of labor, even if the action of the human operative has not been altered, otherwise. What is characteristic of one part of the productive process, in a system, is radiated as an expression of dynamics in the whole.

Thus, through the introduction of relevant new physical principles, the productivity of the economy as a whole has been increased, in just the same general way that the experience of what turned out to be the creation of our U.S.A. has been a dynamic characteristic of the distinction of the U.S. society from European societies of the same stock included among those with us, here.

This enhancement is not limited to the action of production itself. The enhancement of the environment of production also enhances the expressed productivity. The part of the dynamic as a whole, expresses the whole, in the sense that the citizen, whatever else he or she embodies, nonetheless also reflects the dynamic character of the society as a whole.

In general, in production, the increase of the energy-flux-density of the production or comparable action, increases the net productive powers of labor, even if no other change has occurred at the point of production.

For example, among the poor of India and Africa, no significant rate of increase in local productivity, as in farming, can be secured from production; a generation or two of favorable preconditions were needed for that.

However, if we turn our attention to recommended improvements in infrastructure, as through charging the thorium nuclear reactors for developing increased water supplies, there can be a large net increase in net product through factors of basic economic infrastructure.

For example, in the U.S.A., as in Europe, there has been a catastrophic drop in actually productive activity per capita, a shift accompanied by essentially non-productive make-work, paid for out of reduced income for those employed in actually productive work. The shift to lower technologies, as using highly inefficient "free energy" and similar very low-grade power-sources, for alleged "environmental" reasons, has been a prominent part of national economic catastrophes in the U.S.A. and Europe.

A related, implicitly disastrous effect has been the lowering of the productive capacity of the general population through the catastrophic loss of productive skills through increasing emphasis on "alternative" forms of make-work employment.

Or, if we replace hours of commuting lost through congested traffic patterns, or lost through excessive distance travelled, we have tended to increase the net productive powers of labor of that society, even if no other improvement were introduced as a factor.

This applies not only to particular enhancements of such a form; the disposition of the relevant population for adopting such enhancements, is also determining.

Generally, there are two general "dimensions" of culture which tend to shape the relative potential of a population for performance. The variability of the potential among national cultures generally, and among the sub-sectors of national cultures, acts similarly.

In general, increase of the productive powers of labor requires an increase of relative physical-capital intensity, as well as scientific-technological intensity, including improved qualities and degrees of education, and including greater required emphasis on Classical forms of culture, rather than dionysiac revels.

Similarly, the relative price of the element of the national bill of materials, is a relative price which tends to adapt to what the whole requires for it.

## The U.S.A. & Germany: 1877-1890

One of the greatest leaps in national productivity per capita and per square kilometer, occurred in Germany under the leadership of Chancellor Bismarck, between approximately the 1877 aftermath of the U.S.A.'s great Philadelphia Centennial and the ruinous effects of the

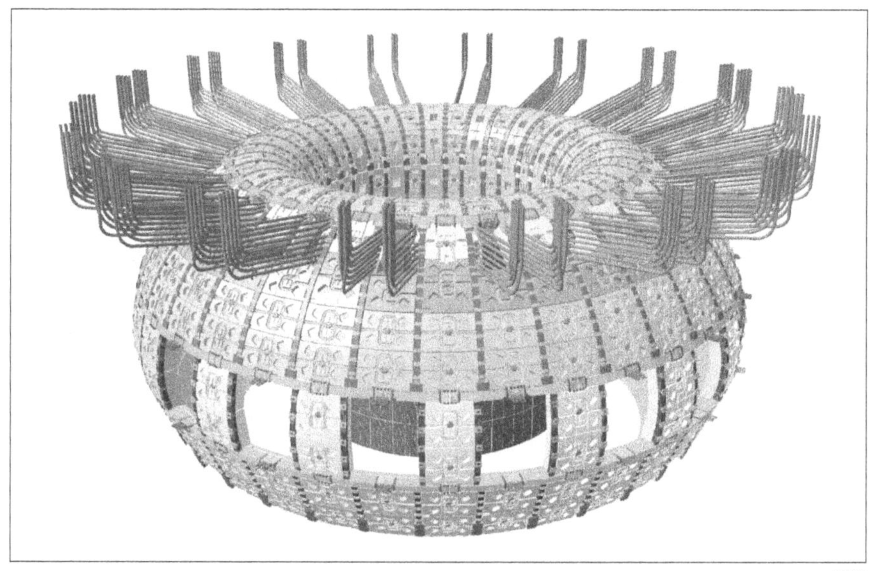

The International Thermonuclear Experimental Reactor (ITER) project: high energy-flux-density power for the 21st Century. Shown is a drawing of the "blanket," which removes heat from the plasma and protects the vacuum vessel and magnets from radiation damage. It is subdvided into modules to allow ease of access.



ouster of Bismarck from the Chancellory. The cause for this progress in Germany was, primarily, the effects of the U.S. victory over the British Empire in the U.S. Civil War of 1861-1865, and the explosion of agro-industrial progress in the U.S.A. during the immediate post-Civil War decade.

Indeed, the cause for what became known as the international wars organized by the British Empire between 1895 (Japan against China) through the close of the first World War, was made possible by the combined effects of the ouster of Bismarck and the assassination of U.S. President William McKinley, enabling the Prince of Wales and later King Edward VII to pit the two cousins, Germany's Kaiser Wilhelm and Russia's Czar Nicholas in war against one another, all for the greater glory of the British Empire.

It was implied that Britain's motive in launching those "Seven-Years-War-like" wars of the 1890-1917 interval was war against transcontinental railway building on the continents of North America and Eurasia. This was, indeed, the keystone motive for all of the wars of the interval, but the more essential issue behind the opposition to transcontinental railways, was that such railway systems shifted the potential power of economies, as measured per capita and per square kilometer, from sea-based, to land-based development, thus undermining the maritime supremacy strategic to the perpetuation of the British empire. Otherwise, that motive of the British financier interest was, as always, and still today, the intent to represent a global financier-imperialist maritime power, to dominate the planet as a whole, forever (it would never succeed, in the end; but they did keep trying).

Thus, the wrecking of the U.S. transcontinental railway system through the promotion of highway motor traffic as a substitute, was, intrinsically, a cause of the ruin of the productivity of the U.S. economy, per capita, and per square kilometer.

In these matters, the physical organization of the economy is essential, but the mental social-cultural organization of the mind and disposition of the population, is even more significant.

EIRNS/Finn Hakansson

The shift to low-grade power sources has been a prominent part of the national economic catastrophes in the U.S.A. and Europe. Here, promotion of ethanol at the New York Stock Exchange, 2006.

## The Issue Is Productivity

In my two most recent webcasts, one of the issues posed as a question from among the participants, was the subject of the benefits of the income of operatives whose source of income was not production. The argument of the question was along the lines of the inherently fraudulent dogma of "marginal utility" introduced in the later Nineteenth Century phase of British imperial perversions.

Ultimately, all true wealth of nations arises from physical-productive output. This is effected either through physical production as such, or as activities which are essential to either that production itself or the households which supply functionally necessary support for the functions of physical production, such as science and engineering, and the essential administration of government and productive enterprises. Marginal utility is sheer bunk.

*A crucial feature of productivity, ignored by British System economists, is individual human scientific and technological creativity. Here, scientist/engineers Thomas Edison and Charles Steinmetz, at a General Electric facility in Schenectady, N.Y., 1922.*

The cult-dogma of "marginal utility" presumes that there is a potential equilibrium between prices of goods or services and the relative "good" which society senses (by some mysterious organ) in a certain ratio of each considered "utility" to the society as a whole. E.g., "cocaine" and "heroin" make some people happy. There is, in fact, no natural money-price which could be equilibriated. U.S.A. and other past experience has shown, that social agreement on a range of "fair trade" prices is the best option for defining price-ranges. There is nothing inhering in that object called a commodity which defines a proper price for it.

There are three principal aspects to national productivity, when that productivity is assessed in terms of those principles of dynamics reflected in this report.

One is at the virtual "point of production." A second is the technology and related capital formation in which the production and circulation of the product is situated. A third is the society in which both the productive individual and that individual's household is situated, and also the physical capital formation invested in both of the previous two aspects of the process. The part reflects, and thus radiates, that which it represents within the whole.

That point is conveniently illustrated by referring to the related point that, contrary to the obscene suggestions of the so-called "globalizers," virtually all good product tends to reflect a national cultural character of the product and its production. So, the World Trade Organization (WTO) is a lunatic venture whose time will never come. Up to eighty percentile of the product consumed in any region of the world should be produced within that region. This rule ensures lowering the net cost and supporting the benefit to the consumer nation.

The corollary of these considerations lies in the nature of the principles of the dynamics of technological progress. On this account, there is, most immediately, the generation and transmission of the relevant advance in technology, and also the technology-intensity of the physical-economic accumulation of both technological capital applied and that consumed. There is the capital-intensive level of accumulated investment in technology in use to be considered, and the rate of capital-intensive and technology intensive productivity and product development to be considered.

A British gentleman once uttered a book on the subject of "the production of commodities by commodities." The author was clever, but essentially mistaken. The subject of a proper book would have been the progress of mankind through the progress of man's scientific-progress-driven, increasingly capital-intensive production of man. Creative progress in the individual human mind's comprehension of the universe, through aid of fundamental scientific progress in rising levels of progress in technological intensity had been a better title, and, hopefully, also better content for a book.

# There the Parallel Is Again: The LaRouche Case and the Suspended Fake Newsman, Brian Ross

Dec. 3 (EIRNS)—On Dec. 1, 2017, as the anti-Trump media mob was in full throat in the United States over Michael Flynn's plea to lying to the FBI, ABC Chief Investigative Reporter Brian Ross let loose a "bombshell." According to his sources, Ross proclaimed, Flynn had already told Special Counsel Robert Mueller that a "high level" official of the Trump campaign had told Flynn to contact the Russians during the 2016 election campaign. The stock market promptly dropped 300 points, as traders digested whether or not the long-lost proof of Russian collusion in the U.S. election had finally come to light.

The problem is that Ross's claim was completely and totally false. Flynn's plea deal specifies that Flynn was asked to contact the Russians—a completely legal activity—after the election. An extremely embarrassed ABC News issued a full retraction and suspended Ross for a month, without pay.

Ross has a history of outright lies and fabrications on behalf of the U.S. intelligence community sources, whose leaks of gossip, lies, and fabrications to him form the bulk of his journalistic *oeuvre*. Like special prosecutor Robert Mueller, Ross cut his teeth on assassination by media falsehood and the U.S. criminal justice system, in the case of Lyndon LaRouche.

Then a reporter for NBC News, Ross played a major role in a campaign of media defamations against LaRouche originating in a salon of journalists run by John Train, a spook long associated with President George H.W. Bush and the CIA. The goal of this salon was to create pariah status for LaRouche through the news media, in order to facilitate a manufactured criminal prosecution against him. LaRouche had terrified the Anglo-American elite by proposing an alternative to their bankrupt system, which was catching on with the U.S. population and with significant foreign leaders. A similar terror today is presented by President Trump's desire to ally with Russia and China to end perpetual war and engage in systemic physical economic development of the world.

In the LaRouche case, among other outrageous defamations the Train crew and Brian Ross invented, in conjunction with U.S. agencies, the claim that LaRouche had plotted to assassinate President Jimmy Carter by remote-controlled bomb, and that LaRouche was involved in the assassination of Olof Palme. The latter fabrication was actually planted on Ross and his fellow hacks by the East German Stasi with collaboration from Mueller's Boston U.S. Attorney's Office.

The full story of the parallels between the LaRouche case and the present coup attempt against the President, and the British intelligence origin of both cases, can be found in the *EIR* Dossier, "Robert Mueller Is an Amoral Assassin, He Will Do His Job If You Let Him."

Like Robert Mueller's well-known prosecutorial excesses and illegalities on behalf of the Anglo-American establishment, Brian Ross has a long and ugly prior record of fake-news reporting. ABC has previously been forced to retract and apologize when Ross claimed that Colorado shooter James Holmes belonged to the Tea Party. In 2001, Ross claimed Saddam Hussein and Iraq were behind the deadly anthrax mailings in the wake of 9/11—juicing the skids, with completely fake reporting, for the disastrous invasion of Iraq. ABC News had to retract again when Ross claimed that a former prisoner from Guantanamo Bay masterminded the underwear terror bombing. The problem with that one, is that the prisoner in question was in full Saudi custody. Then there was the Toyota malfunction story, in which Ross got caught editing and splicing video tape in a fabricated scene of an out-of-control car.

Has the Greek Nemesis principle finally struck in the coup-beleaguered United States? We have yet to see.